Damn Fine
STORY

CHUCK WENDIG

WD

WRITER'S DIGEST
BOOKS

WritersDigest.com
Cincinnati, Ohio

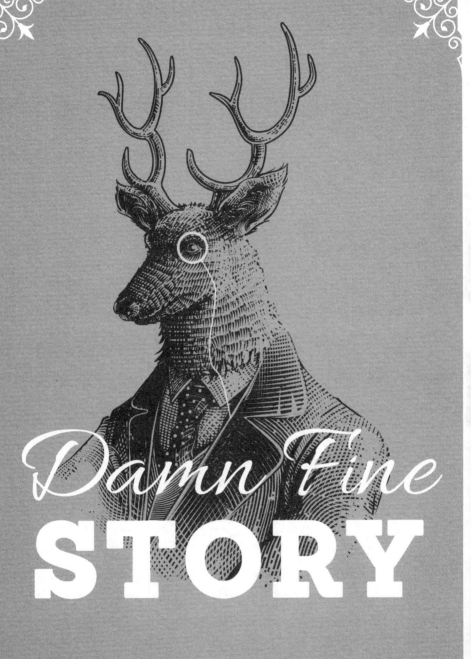

Damn Fine
STORY

MASTERING THE TOOLS OF A POWERFUL NARRATIVE

CHUCK WENDIG

For more resources for writers, visit www.writersdigest.com.

21 20 19 18 17   5 4 3 2

Distributed in Canada by Fraser Direct
100 Armstrong Avenue
Georgetown, Ontario, Canada L7G 5S4
Tel: (905) 877-4411

Distributed in the U.K. and Europe by F+W Media International
Pynes Hill Court, Pynes Hill, Rydon Lane
Exeter, EX2 5AZ, United Kingdom
Tel: (+44) 1392-797680, Fax: (+44) 1626-323319
E-mail: postmaster@davidandcharles.co.uk

Library of Congress Cataloging-in-Publication Data

ISBN-13: 978-1-4403-4838-9

Edited by Karen Krumpak
Designed by Alexis Estoye
Production coordinated by Debbie Thomas

DEDICATION

To Margaret Atwood, for being kind enough to diminish her own literary legacy in recommending my foul-mouthed blog and unsavory writing advice to those who ask.

And to my father, who is the blood and beating heart of not only a lot of the stories in this book, but also of why I tell stories in the first damn place.

ACKNOWLEDGMENTS

First and foremost, I have to acknowledge all the readers who come to terribleminds.com—though the blog is ostensibly for me and about me first and foremost, they press me and challenge me with great questions, comments, and ideas, and have only helped refine how I look about writing and storytelling—and further, how I *communicate* my thoughts about writing and storytelling.

I also need to thank a lot of the writer-friends (originally mistyped as "writer-fiends," and I nearly left it that way) who have appeared at the blog over the years: Delilah Dawson, Adam Christopher, Andrea Phillips, Elsa Sjunneson-Henry, Kevin Hearne, Stephen Blackmoore, and others.

Thanks too to Phil Sexton at Writer's Digest for helping me get this book out into the world, and my agent, Stacia Decker, for getting it into his hands in the first place.

Finally, thanks to Stephen King for *On Writing*.

Because, c'mon.

C'mon.

kisses fingers

ABOUT THE AUTHOR

 Chuck Wendig is the New York Times best-selling author of *Star Wars: Aftermath*, as well as the Miriam Black thrillers, the Atlanta Burns books, and the Heartland YA series, alongside other works across comics, games, film, and more. A finalist for the John W. Campbell Award for Best New Writer and the cowriter of the Emmy-nominated digital narrative *Collapsus*, he is also known for his popular blog, terribleminds.com, and his books about writing. He lives in Pennsylvania with his family.

TABLE *of* CONTENTS

INTRODUCTION

My father never read a book. At least, I never saw him read one. He had books on his shelves, mostly books about cowboys and a lot of books about guns (price guides, catalogs, gunsmithing and reloading manuals). But that was it. I never saw him sit down and read a book the way most of you do—and the way I certainly do every day.

He never read a book, but he always told stories.

Every day, a story to tell. Some were new stories, like the one he told after he had played a prank on a co-worker: The guys at the plant always bought lottery tickets, right? Dreams of a bigger future and all that. One of the guys came to my dad and asked him to read off the winning lottery numbers to compare to his ticket. As he read those numbers off and they matched, one by one, the eyes of his co-worker (who we'll call Dave) grew bigger and bigger with every number, until the time came when he realized he'd won. He'd won it *all*. The big prize, the epic payout. And already he started conspiring about who he'd *not* give money to, what he'd buy, what it would be like to be a man of great wealth. He'd tell them to screw this job to hell, and he'd walk right outta there, goddamnit—

Of course, my father already knew Dave's numbers, having snuck a look at the man's tickets in advance, and was able to list those numbers off one by one—his poker face not giving any tells to the fact he was pranking the poor bastard. So, eventually, Dave realized what was happening and *ha ha ha*, poor Dave, who was no longer going to screw this job, who wouldn't get the chance to cut out greedy relatives, who wouldn't learn what it was to be a man of great wealth after all.

Sometimes the stories were older stories.

Like the time he caught fire.

Or the other time, where he got into a huge riot-sized fight at a Phillies game.

Or about the time he lost his pinky finger.

Most of that finger was indeed gone, missing down below the middle knuckle. The stub had two black dots like a pair of little eyes looking up from its center. Way Dad told it was this: He was operating a log-splitter, and one log crashed into another log, with his pinky caught between them. It mashed his pinky to a red paste.

Now, if I did that, I'd likely spend a lot of time rolling around on the ground and screaming, but my father—stoic as a carpentry nail—idolized John Wayne, so he just saddled himself up into his pickup and drove off to the hospital.

As the story goes, he went into the hospital and saw the doctor, and the doctor said, "That finger has to go." No saving it. It wasn't Play-Doh—you couldn't sculpt it into something finger-shaped and call it a day. (Maybe nowadays you could, but this was in the 1970s.) My father, notoriously thrifty, wanted to know the cost of said finger-removal service. The doctor told him, and he found that price unacceptable. He was a practiced haggler, but even he knew you couldn't really haggle with the hospital.

"Hold on," he told the doc. Then he walked out of the room, out of the hospital, and to his truck. He pulled out a toolbox from the back of the truck, and from that toolbox he procured a pair of bolt cutters.

And then he cut his own pinky off.[1]

After that, he walked back into the hospital and had them do the rest—bandaging, cauterizing, whatever. He paid a lesser bill, having done the "hard work" for them. Then he went home and got back to work.

This is merely a sampling of his stories. Every day, he told some kind of story just like we all do. He might tell us what happened on the way home from work; something his own father did; that time he jumped a creek bed in a snowmobile with my mother riding on the back, and they flipped and somehow didn't get a scratch on them; that time he got lost in the Colorado wilderness while hunting an elk. On and on, story after story.

And they were riveting.

He knew the cadence of storytelling. He had a feel for hooking you with the promise of something interesting, and then there was always a little twist, a little turn. He presented the tales just right, *just so*, like the perfect bowl of porridge in the bear cottage. He didn't keep you waiting too long, but he didn't blurt it all out, either. My father had a natural sense of how narratives rise and fall, and how to keep his audience interested.

Dad knew how to tell a damn fine story.

. . . . .

This is not a book of writing advice.

It's not here to help make you a better writer. Rather, it's here to help you become a better *storyteller*.

---

[1] (He'd often torment children with the pinky finger. He'd hold up one of his still-complete fingers and say "pull my finger," except instead of ripping a beefy fart, he'd quickly switch to the pinky finger and scream, making the children think they had, in fact, pulled off half of his finger.)

Nothing wrong with writing advice. It is necessary to know where the comma goes, and how sentence construction works to create pace and rhythm, and how to know the rules in order to break them *and* to break the rules in order to know why we needed them in the first damn place. Writing is a vital, elegant mechanism—but it's not the reason we do what we do, or at least not most of us. Writing isn't just for the pretty words, or for the well-constructed sentences, or for the way the poetry of it looks in our mind's eye and sounds in our mind's ear.[2] Writing is a means to an end.

Writing is a *delivery system*.

And what it delivers is, in part, stories. Writing can deliver truth and lies, it can deliver ideas, it can transmit dreams and nightmares, but, for our purposes, for the creation of fiction, it conveys all these things through *story*. Writing is a craft-driven procedure with rules, though certainly it has a lot of flexibility built in.

Storytelling is a whole different animal and demands different butchery. It's art as much as craft. It's intuition more than law. Writing is a road we build, but storytelling is a river—it's bendy and strange and hard to predict. It's natural, too, part of our psychic and social landscape. It's why we sometimes feel like our stories and the characters in those stories are not precisely in our control, like we are no more than an antenna receiving narrative signals from some funky tale-spinning trickster god out there in the galaxy. We speak of *inspiration* and *muses* like they're exterior forces and we're just their puppets. The truth is far more crass and crafty, I find: If you wait for inspiration to show up, you'll never get the work done. Sometimes you just have to start telling the story. The act of writing, of telling the tale, is also the act of laying traps. And it is in these traps that we capture our muses. In other words, we capture *them*, they don't capture *us*.

I've had the good fortune in my career to have written across a variety of media. I've written a bunch of books, some comics, a

---

[2] Is that a thing? The mind's ear? It is now, so shut up.

handful of film and TV scripts (including a short film that premiered at Sundance and a digital narrative called *Collapsus*). Each of these formats presents story in its own persnickety way. Film has its half-bullshit, half-not-bullshit three-act structure. TV has multiple acts based on the number of commercial breaks punctuating the tale, and ending those acts is a practice of fish-hooking the viewer so they stay through, and return *after*, the commercial break. A novel is an unruly, brutish beast—big as a brick and often quite stubborn in its independence. The comic book format is what would happen if a TV show and a novel had an ink-stained, four-color baby: It offers the visual and episodic dimension of a television show, but the internal, character-driven dimension of a novel. I've even written games, which is often about empowering players to act as proxy protagonists, telling their own stories using the LEGO bricks chosen for the experience.

Each format is different. One is not easily made into the other. You can't just cram a film into a comic book (trust me, I've tried, and it's harder than passing a cantaloupe through your urethra). A novel is often too sprawling for a film, and a short story is probably too *short*.

And yet, each format has its similarities, too. The more you work across the spectrum of story modes, the more you see these similarities emerge, like languages that all come from a single "ur-source."[3] Because stories are stories. Stories have *bones* that they share, even if over time they evolve new flappy limbs and orifices and flesh nubbins. Stories have a sense of shared architecture—okay, sure, a mansion is not a houseboat, and a houseboat is not a rancher, and a rancher is not a Cape Cod, but each structure serves similar needs. You still get your bedrooms and your kitchens. You still have water and electricity, pipes and conduits. You still have corners, win-

---

[3] An ur-source is based on the Germanic prefix *ur*, meaning original, or first. So, this refers to an ultimate, originating source.

dows, doors. Just like story, you may have different shapes, different expressions, but you still get your corners and windows and doors.

Our goal here is to find those common corners and those shared windows and doors. The hope is to learn how to not just tell a story, but how to tell a *damn fine* one.

Put differently, and to reiterate what I said at the fore:

My father never read books. He certainly never wrote one.

But he could tell a damn fine story.

And you can, too.

CAVEATS

Before we begin, some things I ask you to understand.

First point:

Though this is not precisely a book of *writing* advice, it is a book about the art and the craft of storytelling.

It isn't about having answers. Because I don't have the answers. This isn't science. This isn't math. You can't plug a bunch of narrative components into an equation and spit out a perfect story. The truth is, most of what I'm telling you here is wildly imperfect. It's guesswork. It's lies layered with horseshit layered with I-don't-know-what-I'm-talking-about. You don't have the answers, either.

Now, *writing* is beholden to very specific rules, and though these rules are very flexible, they are also teachable. The comma goes here. The sentence ends there.

Storytelling is far more … *wiggly.*

The goal of this book is not to provide you with answers but, rather, to force you to consider the questions. I want you to ask about your own work and the stories you've read/watched/played. I want to challenge you with ideas, old and new. Some of this book will help you. Other parts will be worthless to you. Discard what you find distasteful, and hold the rest to your chest like a beloved child. Do whatever works. But just know that this is not a hard and fast process. None of this is about answers carved in stone.[1]

Second point:

This book makes use of many well-known stories as references; for the most part, I use movies, and occasionally comics and books. The reason I'm using Very Popular Pop Media as my touchstone is because, well, we *need* a touchstone. I can't go spouting off about My Favorite Book because maybe you haven't read it. And even if *you* have, those ten other people over there have not. You are far likelier to have seen *Die Hard* or *The Empire Strikes Back* than to have read some old, out-of-print horror novel, for instance, and so Very Popular Pop Media tends to be more dominant in terms of the references I offer.

… Also, that means I spoil them more than a little.

So, enter with wary eyes! I won't be spoiling anything *new*—it's not like I'll be ruining last week's episode of That Show You Love or *Star Wars: Episode XVI*[2] or whatever.

Stay frosty. Ever vigilant. For *thar be spoilers in these here waters.*

Third and final point:

I use bad language.

On my blog—cough, cough, terribleminds.com—it's worse. But even so, this is a book that contains adult language. I mean, it's not the Kama Sutra or anything, but it occasionally gets a wee little bit naughty.

You are forewarned. The strong spice of vulgarity is present—some have a taste for it; others do not.

Let us begin.

---

[1] Real talk time? A lot of writing, storytelling, and even publishing advice is bullshit—but never forget, bullshit fertilizes. Ideas have value to those who can use them. So even if I just make you challenge or reconsider your processes without adopting the specific pieces of advice, hey, I'd call that a win.

[2] Snoke is Rey's mother, and Rey is Snoke's father. And Chewbacca is really just three Ewoks stacked on top of each other.

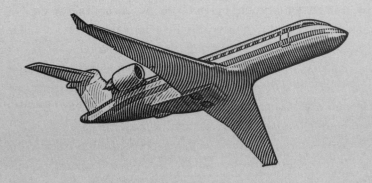

Interlude

THE FIRST RULE

The first rule of Story Club is that we don't talk about Story Club.

That doesn't sound right.

checks notes

Ah! That's *Fight* Club. Sorry, sorry. My bad.

The first rule of Story Club is—

Wait wait wait. First, let's talk about that word, *rule*. Writing has rules, and storytelling has … nnnyeah, not-quite-rules. It has suggestions. It has theories. It has principles and precepts that ideally govern the flow of narrative, even as narrative bends like a snake away from such defined ideas. Stories have very few hard-and-fast rules of note, though. One suspects there must exist a beginning, a middle, and an end, and certainly key components are expected to be in place: character, setting, and so forth.

Beyond that, the laws of storytelling are not so much chiseled in stone as they are drawn with a toothpick in a quivering slab of Jell-O. And yet, for the context of this book, we still need a baseline. We need some aspects of Story-with-a-capital-S that are at least commonly understood, if not indefatigably irrefutable.

And so, throughout this book, you will find these interstitial interludes,[1] and these interstices will attempt to establish that baseline with some hard-and-fast rules.[2] Here, then, is the first rule:

Storytelling is an act of interrupting the status quo.

What I mean is this: A story's very existence is predicated on its divergence, from some or all of the storyworld's existing conditions and circumstances ("storyworld" being fancy writer talk for the overall setting and cast of characters, and the narrative rules that govern those people and that space).

When we tell a story, it's because something has changed. If we can imagine narrative as a line, then the story *begins* when something bends, twists, or sharply breaks that line. The life of Bruce Wayne is a straight line: A rich kid has a rich family and everything's fine. And then the line is sliced in twain as a robber kills both of his parents—and it's Batman who emerges from that grim fissure in Bruce Wayne's timeline. Katniss in The Hunger Games series lives in a dystopian nightmare—but even still, one that is given over to the status quo of *that* dystopian nightmare—and then one day it all changes when her sister is called to an annual televised event called *The Hunger Games.* Katniss responds to that turn of the status quo with her own twist and replaces her sister, thus deepening the divide between what was formerly "normal" and what is now irreversibly transformed.

Die Hard immediately gives us a number of signals that demonstrate a shattered status quo. New York cop in sunny California?

---

[1] You'll also find footnotes. Like this one. See? Footnote. This is a footnote. It is not a note on your foot. It is a note at the bottom of the page. The foot of the page? Pagefeet? Words are weird.

[2] Or at least, erm, *harder-and-faster.*

There's one. On a plane flight when he hates flying? Another. Bringing a gun on a flight, earning him strange looks? The hits keep on coming. None of this is normal. All of these diverge from our expectation. But the big ones are yet to come—first, that it's Christmas (holidays are themselves a kind of break in the status quo); second, that he is in the middle of a divorce (a divorce is a very literal break in the narrative line of till-death-do-us-part marriage); third, that *oh yeah*, he's about to be trapped in a skyscraper attacked by a gang of terrorists-who-are-really-thieves.

In *Star Wars: A New Hope*, it's another bundle of status quo interruptions. A rude princess interrupts the lovely starship ride of two droids and sends them on a new mission. Throw in a sand-crusted farm boy who gets swept up in that mission and, for Luke, the hits to the status quo are literally part of his quest. He wants his life to change, and oh, change it does! He meets Old Wizard Ben. His Uncle Owen and Aunt Beru become Jawa barbecue. Then he meets a smuggler and his walking carpet co-pilot, and it's time to leave home, and so on. Star Wars as a saga shows us how a story isn't just about one status quo change, but about several. Often, just as a narrative grows comfortable and starts to settle into a straight line, it disrupts itself again. It's like a plane flight you think is going smoothly, but every time you grow comfortable in your seat, here comes the turbulence yet again to keep you awake. The status quo keeps changing in the Star Wars story: Luke discovering who his father is, then who his sister is; Obi-Wan's death, then Yoda's; the destruction of not one but two Death Stars. It's this latter point that shows us that the interruption or obliteration of the status quo is not necessarily for the protagonist alone: Darth Vader loses the precious Death Star plans *and* discovers he has a son and a daughter. And with these things, the Empire sees its paradigm change. In that saga, the whole of the galaxy is subject to the kind of narrative turbulence I'm talking about—

And it's the entire reason the story exists.

Stories begin when things change.

The change might be a death or a divorce. It might be a cataclysm that's quiet and personal, or one that's global or even galactic. It's a storm, a betrayal, a loss, a gain. Story is like a broken bone: With it comes pain, but also the chance for growth. And it gives us reason to howl to the heavens.

Stories are about change.

Consider that the first rule.

Chapter One

STORY IS, STORY AS

I had a debate teacher once, and part of his deal was to endlessly hound us on a single point:

Define your terms.

If you were going to make a point—or, more important, refute someone else's—then you had to make it clear what you were talking about *precisely*, so that there could be no doubt of your message.

It's also an idea that holds true when you're writing a thesis paper—whether that thesis paper is about the unstable geopolitics of North Freedonia or how the mating habits of the unruly puffin helped spawn Western civilization, you have to be clear about every aspect of what you're trying to say. You have to define your damn terms.

And so, it seems like a good idea to try to define my terms.

Which means, up front, I need to define the biggest term of all: STORY.

One problem, though. Story evades definition. Perhaps because, as I noted earlier, so few rules actually govern the act of storytelling, the very idea of *story* escapes just as you try to define it. It's like a greased-up python—it'll always squirm and slip from your grip, just as you think you've got a good hold on the thing. Saying that "story is this" or "story is that" is a very good way to invite a dump truck full of exceptions to the rule. You will be buried in them. For every supposed rule that exists in storytelling, countless deviations also exist.

Instead of focusing on a single definition, let's look at story through a series of lenses, each framing story in a different way—not to give us one *perfect* view of what storytelling is and how it works, but rather, to see it multiple ways, from multiple angles, to give us a larger, broader, and altogether *weirder* view of narrative and how we create it, evolve it, and share it.

STORY SHAPES

Two words: Freytag's Pyramid.

Nope, it's not the strange occult store that just moved in at the edge of town. Nor is it a game show, the new drug all the kids are doing, or a kinky sex move.[1] Rather, it's a visual device to help you grasp the rough shape of narrative. The shape is, well, a *pyramid*. At the base of the pyramid, you have exposition, or the information you need to know to get into the story. On the left side of the pyramid, you get rising action, which is the part where, simplistically put, stuff is beginning to happen. At its peak is the climax—the whiz-bang coming-together of all the tale elements!—and then it sinks back down the far side with falling action and denouement. Events slow as the bits of the story are all tied up. All is concluded.

---

[1] Though maybe it *should* be a kinky sex move.

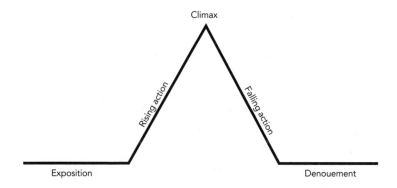

Freytag's Pyramid is also bullshit.

I mean, it's not *bullshit*-bullshit, okay? Of course it gets a few things right: Most stories do have a rise to action, a climax, and then a conclusion, but that's not really all that different from saying a story has a beginning, a middle, and an end. It's a nice bit of visualization to see the story as a mountain one must climb, true, but at the same time, that single shape is woefully limited and overly simplistic.

No story conforms to a standard shape.

A story might look more like a jagged mountain. Each individual peak, of which there can be many of varying heights and angles, illustrates a rise-to-and-fall-from-climax in miniature. At every peak, you thin out the oxygen, and in every valley, you breathe more oxygen in. Each peak of the mountain is higher than the one before it, thus creating an overall sense of upward momentum—the same momentum indicated by Freytag's Cough-Cough-Mostly-Bullshit Pyramid, but with greater nuance.

Of course, even the Jaggedy-Toothed Mountain shape is bullshit, too, because stories aren't really two-dimensional. It may offer you a good start, but it's not necessarily enough to convey the overall movement of the narrative. If you think about story in a *three-dimensional* way, suddenly you get a roller coaster—it rises, it falls, it whips left, it jerks right, it corkscrews through the air before spinning you upside down in a vicious loop de loop. And then it slows and the ride is over. Isn't that how a story looks, sometimes? Or better yet, how a story *feels*? A two-dimensional variant assumes the tale is predictable in its inevitable ascent, however herky-jerky it might seem. A roller coaster, though, is full of surprises, offering twists and turns that all fit together as part of one track. Some roller coasters are faster and scarier. Some are slower, with gentler curves. Consider the shape of every roller coaster and how each might reflect a different story.

STORY AS A HOUSE

We use the metaphor of architecture a lot when talking about narrative, and it's appropriate because, as with the roller coaster, architecture is more than a two-dimensional blueprint. Architecture is three-dimensional. It has space—and, in a sense, it has time, too, as we move through it (which I think makes it demonstrative of the *fourth* dimension).

More specifically, though, consider story as a *house*.

Just as story is not one thing, neither is a house one thing. You think of a house, and you may think of a Cape Cod, or a rancher, or the haunted sprawl of the Winchester Mansion, or one of those fancy "tiny houses."[2] A house is a house is a house, just as a story is a story is a story, regardless of the variance in their shapes.

You could argue that the more two-dimensional representations of narrative (like Freytag's Half-Ass Triangle) are more emblematic of *plot* than they are of *story*. And here, it's vital to understand the differences between those two things, once again seeking to (as my debate teacher roars at me from inside my own memories) DEFINE OUR TERMS.

---

[2] Those tiny house shows are an addiction of mine, by the way. An easy drinking game is to take a drink every time a prospective buyer seems surprised that the tiny house is, *gasp*, tiny. You'll be black-out drunk after one episode.

I am fond of saying that story is an apple and plot is the arrow through the apple. Meaning, story is the whole picture, whereas plot is merely our path through the picture. Plot is our sequence of events, the steps by which we experience the story. But the story is bigger, unrulier—a much roomier entity than the plot itself. Apple versus arrow. Or, if you want a more meandering sequence of events (one that is not so much a straight line) think of the worm's path through the apple as the plot, a worm drunk on fermented juice, zigzagging his way through fruit flesh. The fact that this is a "path" matters here because it means plot is not *merely* the sequence of events, but rather the sequence of events as revealed to the audience. It's how they experience moving through those events—it is in how you arrange them.

If we think of story as a house, then our path through the house is the plot. It is the steps the audience takes when led through the space.

In a sense, the reverse is also true: If we see a story as a house, it's worth seeing how a house is also a story. Meaning, if you take someone's actual home, and you break into their house and wander through it like a nosy tiptoeing tourist, the house will offer up the story of both the people who live there and, perhaps, its own architectural narrative. On the architecture front you might say, "Ah, this is an American Craftsman-style home with a gabled roof and the exposed beams and the preponderance of stone and wood, and I would guess that it was built in the 1920s." But as you looked deeper, as you poked through the refrigerator and the medicine cabinets and the dresser drawers, you'd get a picture of the characters who live there. (Vegan food, vitamins, and sex toys! Empty fridge, Xanax, and punk T-shirts! Leftovers, pain meds, and unused yoga pants!) You'd look at the walls and see photos of the family, and that would tell a story, too—Timmy used to play soccer, now he's playing baseball; Dad's in the early photos and now he's not, which means either death or divorce. The photos might reveal a series of dogs.[3] Of course, if you were allowed to open the homeowner's computer or phone, or find

---

[3] It was George Carlin who famously said, "Life is a series of dogs."

the shoebox of old letters and Polaroids under the bed, you'd see a deeper, more secret story. You'd find e-mails and text messages and love letters that reveal a hidden side to these people—and that would lead you to realize that some parts of a house are a public story, and other parts contain a private, secret story. When you enter a house, some of it has been sanitized for you, the stranger. Other parts are meant to be inaccessible, hidden behind passwords or in lockboxes.

Then you wonder, what else can't you see?

And so we come back to how a story is like a house.

A story reveals itself in pieces, just as a house does: Exposition moves us from the public to the private, though we may see hints of the private early on (an overdue bill on the table, a half-empty bottle of bourbon on the counter, a naked dead guy on the living room couch). Deeper into the house and deeper into the story, we gain access to secrets—we see the public veneer of family photos peeled away to reveal problems (drug habits, an affair, a father's anger issues). It takes us from *text*, or what's on the surface, to *subtext*, or what the house has tried to hide. We move through the house, ascending stairs and entering rooms that are meant to be locked.

And other things remain hidden, too.

Just as a house keeps much of its own infrastructure hidden from view, so too does a story keep *its* infrastructure concealed. Behind the walls in a house you'll find pipes and wires and ducts. And behind the walls of a story you'll find theme, motivation, ideas, and other unspoken literary devices that feed the story invisibly. And the decor of a house is like the mood of the tale at hand: A house might have bright paint, new furniture, clean floors. Or it might have water stains on the ceiling, roaches running about, and rot in the corners. The house has its own *feel*, just as a story does—and a story exhibits this feel through things like word choice, imagery, metaphor, and motif.

A story has characters just as a house has occupants and visitors.

A story has plot just as a house has our path through it.

A story has secrets, and so does a house.

When you tell a story, think about how it mirrors a journey through a house. A house, perhaps, into which we were uninvited. A house where something is wrong, where we have been compelled to enter by dint of a broken window, or blood on a doorknob, or the sounds of a struggle within. Think about moving through the house, exploring its broader spaces and then its nooks and crannies—and how that parallels the telling of a story, the exploration of a story's larger spaces and then the smaller, more forbidden ones, too.

In terms of narrative arrangement, a storyteller first reveals those things that visitors to the house would see right away: the obvious elements. The visitors would see a house in obvious disarray. They would see the doorways and the windows. And then, as they move through the space, they might begin to follow the trail of mysteries. What caused the disarray? What can be seen through the windows or be visited by entering through the doors? Visitors will chase these mysteries.

With enough time and thorough wandering, a house will reveal to guests its mysteries and then give up its truths. And so will a story. Your readers are your guests, after all.

THE MAGIC TRICK

We like to think of storytelling as actual magic. Like we have a little wizard or witch hiding in our heart, and *she's* the one who's barfing inspiration into us—where we then translate that magical inspiration-barf to our fingertips as we write or to our jabbering mouth-hole as we in turn regurgitate the tale at hand.

Hell with that. Writing and storytelling aren't magic, even when they seem to be. We control them. There are no wizards, no witches. No Muse exists to fuel our whimsy.

Think of us instead as *stage magicians*.

Stage magic, magic tricks, illusions—they work a certain way. There exists a narrative to every trick, a beginning, a middle, and an end, just as in a story. And the stage magician does not make these up willy-nilly out of nowhere. They are articulated, designed, and practiced endlessly, until they are worth taking to the stage and, by proxy, the audience beyond it. This isn't entirely different from how we create more formalized stories, right? We write them down. Some of us plan and outline them. And even when we don't, that first draft isn't the final draft (or, ahem, *it damn well shouldn't be*). We iterate and reiterate. We do a second draft, a third, a seventh, we create as many drafts as it takes to get the story—the magic, the trick, the illusion!—just right.

So, a trick has a beginning, a middle, and an end. Christopher Priest, in his book *The Prestige*, calls this "the Pledge, the Turn, and the Prestige." Just as many films have three acts, so too does each bit of stage magic.

The beginning establishes the status quo of the trick: Behold, here is a hat, a box, a chicken, my Grandpa Gary, whatever. The trick even attempts to establish the normalcy, the *reality*, of what you're seeing. The magician shows you the inside of the box. He taps the bottom of the hat and puts it on his head. He lets the chicken squawk or leans in so you can hear Grandpa Gary snoring and farting in his sleep. "Look," the magician says. "All is normal, all is well, all is as expected." Implicit in this is the subtext, "And now I'm going to disrupt it all to hell." This is the Pledge.

The middle is the flourish, the Turn. It's a twist, a change of state in the way that one could turn liquid to gas. It is an elemental shift. A rabbit is out of the hat, a woman in the box disappears, the chicken is now a dog, Grandpa Gary is now dismembered with his still-flailing octogenarian limbs cast about the stage like so much kindling. The stage magician has not only ended the status quo, the magician has, in a sense, *broken reality itself.* The rules you thought you knew (rabbits can't appear out of nowhere, people can't disappear, grandpas cannot be chopped into bits and remain alive) are way out the window, bye-bye.

The final act of the trick is, in a sense, like the final act of a hero's journey—the hero must return from his adventure, the same but changed, and so too must the rabbit go back into the hat. The woman must reappear. The dog once again becomes chicken. Grandpa Gary is whirled about and, in a flash, all his limbs are mysteriously unsevered, and he's free to go back to sleep. As Priest explains in *The Prestige*, "Making something disappear isn't enough; you have to bring it back."

A magic trick, then, is the ultimate act of performative trolling: The magician shows you the world, breaks your world, and then puts it back together again. But you, the audience, are left with the suspicion that what you thought you knew is wrong. *Now* you fear everything is fragile, and the status quo can change with the snap of the magician's fingers.

Speaking of the snap of the magician's fingers—

There exists another vital component to the magic trick.

It is this: *misdirection.*

To repeat: Stage magic is not real magic. A rabbit is not literally appearing out of nowhere. Grandpa Gary is not literally being dismembered. It's a trick. *A ruse.* And in order for it to work, it has to feel real. We can't see the wires or the mirrors. Seeing the secret compartment where the rabbit hides will cause our disbelief to flare up like a bad case of herpes. We will begin to *doubt*, and doubt ruins the fun. (Just as it does with a story.)

To cover up the truth of the trick—to hide the mechanism—the stage magician must do something to distract you. Or, more correctly, he must misdirect you, turning your attention away from the mechanism and to some other, innocuous detail. Misdirection may be happening as early as the first part of the trick, organically folded into the act of demonstrating the normalcy and the status quo. As he shows you the hat, spinning it around, putting it on his head, tapping it inside and out, he's misdirecting you. While *you* are focused on the hat, the magician is expertly preparing the release of the rabbit from whatever Secret Rabbit Chamber exists on the magician's body (from a pocket sewn into his vest, perhaps, or, I dunno, from up the magician's own ass).

The question becomes, then, how is stage magic like a story?

BEHOLD AS I PULL THE NARRATIVE RABBIT OUT OF THIS METAPHORICAL HAT—AND DEFINITELY NOT MY ASS.[4]

A story, as noted, is about the breaking of the status quo. The story shows us The Way Things Are, then it reveals the truth about them. It demonstrates a secret. Or a lie. Or it breaks the thing we (and the characters inside the story) assumed to be safe. Then, at the end, it concludes—it returns things to the way they were, or at least to *some* kind of status quo in the world.

It's probably best not to think of your story as being a singular magic trick, though: Rather, it is a collection of them. The story, especially a longer-form tale like a screenplay or a novel, demonstrates an entire *show* of stage magic, a series of escalating tricks that get more bold and more brazen, even building off one another to produce a jaw-dropping, pants-shellacking, climactic finale.

And, just as with the illusion, misdirection is key.

What fun would a murder mystery be if the murderer was plain to see up front? Mystery relies on feeding us options and opportuni-

---

[4] Spoiler warning: It might be out of my own ass. (I mean, not literally, because ew.)

ties for guessing right—and guessing *way* wrong. A red herring is the literary technique of boldly played misdirection—the origin of the idiom is that, if you wanted to get hounds off your scent, you could use the skin of a red herring to draw their attention, thus drawing them away from their actual target.[5]

Consider the misdirection of *A New Hope*, where we're told by a theoretically reputable mentor (Obi-Wan) that Luke's father died in the Clone Wars, killed by Darth Vader. It *is* true (say it with me: *from a certain point of view*, in that Anakin was once a human who was reduced in such a way to be taken over and even destroyed by the Vader persona). It's also a very good way to distract us from the full truth, which is of course that Darth Vader is actually Luke Sky-walker's Uncle Owen, now an undead zombie.[6]

A story doesn't even require a core mystery component to utilize misdirection. In *Die Hard*, Hans Gruber misdirects both the audience and the other characters by simply *lying*—he says that he is a political terrorist acting out of principle, when really what he means is, "The only principle we hold dear is greed, because we're thieves."

The movie further misdirects us about the effectiveness of the police and the order (disorder, really) of the FBI. The story feints, going a different way than you expect. You don't think McClane is going to dump a body on top of a police cruiser because that's just not a thing people do. Sometimes misdirection is simply the act of letting the status quo inform the expectations of the audience. If the audience only knows turning left, going right will be a shock and a revelation. If the audience only knows rogue cops *not* throwing corpses onto patrol cars—well, you get the idea.

The point is, that's how we can generate surprise.

---

[5] I sometimes play a game of misdirection with my son: If I'm trying to tickle him, I move in with the left hand, and as he's trying to fight that one off, I go in with the right. Works every time. Of course, he's five, and if this still works on him when he's thirty, we've got a problem. Also, it's probably weird if I'm still trying to tickle him when he's thirty, so there's that.

[6] Turns out, that's incorrect—apparently, Darth Vader is Luke's Dad? Whoa.

The rabbit's here, the lady's gone, Grandpa Gary is in pieces. Story as stage magic.

Et voila!

THE JOKE

My son, whom we call B-Dub, became aware of the concept of a "joke" a little over a year ago, when he was around four years old. We were sitting at a diner, and he said, "I want to tell you a joke."

My wife and I looked at each other with curiosity and surprise. Note that every day with a small child is like that scene in *Jurassic Park* where the velociraptors learn to open doors. The boy suddenly telling us that he knew what a joke was—well, that was new. It is, in a sense, a formative instance of him not just being funny, but trying to be funny in a mechanical way. Plus, jokes are themselves ministories, so this was exciting. We said, "Sure, go for it."

B-Dub's joke was …

… drumroll please …

"Daddy, you poop fire out of your butt."

Pause.

Beat.

Rimshot, cymbal crash, sad trombone.

That was it. That was the joke.

Now, to be fair, it's pretty much the perfect joke for a four-year-old. Does it have poop? Check. Does it have butt? Check. No pee, but okay, that can be forgiven because at least you get *fire*, and I guess fire is funny? It's not so much funny for me, because I was the one apparently pooping said fire, and as a person who has in his past eaten too much Taco Bell,[7] I can assure you: Pooping fire is no joke.

Still, I thought, here's an opportunity to explain to my son about jokes. I said, "Jokes have a certain format, and at their simplest level

---

[7] You don't "eat" Taco Bell so much as you "rent" it, and then return it to its natural habitat.

are questions you ask that have a funny answer." Then I gave what is arguably the most classic, and also the utter worst, joke ever:

Why did the chicken cross the road?

To get to the other side.

I'm never really sure if the chicken crossing the road is one of those so-called "anti-jokes,"[8] or if it's funny because it plays off "the other side" as a pun. Meaning, the chicken crosses the road and gets hit by a car, thus fulfilling its avian destiny of getting to some kind of chicken-friendly heaven.

Either way, my son didn't laugh, but he got the general idea. And we also went through knock-knock jokes, another concept that's easy to explain—*you knock on the door and someone funny is on the other side, and also, there's wordplay?*—but is harder to teach in execution.

B-Dub said he wanted to try again.

He had a new joke, he explained.

"Go ahead," we said, eager to see what would come out of his mouth.

"*Why* did Daddy poop fire out of his butt?" B-Dub asked.

We gave the call-and-response refrain: "Why?"

"Because the chicken crossed the road."

Aaaaaand that was his joke.

It doesn't make any sense but, hey, some jokes don't have to make sense. And at least he got the format right!

A joke ostensibly works like a magic trick: Whether it's a knock-knock joke or a longer joke or even a whole comedy routine, you set up expectations about the world and then you (once again) twist out of the grip that holds you and screw up the status quo. This time, though, the subversion of the status quo is meant to be funny, ironic, or somehow absurd.

---

[8] An "anti-joke" is a joke that is funny because it's not funny.

A joke *is* a story. A very short story, with just one or two zigzags before the climax. It has no falling action, no denouement.[9]

But some of the things that work for jokes work for larger stories, too, even if those stories aren't supposed to be funny.

First, as said, a joke needs to be short. The longer it goes, the more it rambles, the less effective it is. A joke works because the listener has very little to keep track of—the details are all right there in the setup, no abacus or spreadsheet necessary. Stories can often ramble, stray, and become confusing. Clarity is king in a story. We want to be able to keep track of it all.

Second, a joke leaves a lot *unsaid*. It works because it plays off of things we already understand about the world. We know what a bar is. We understand people knocking at doors. We grok apples and oranges and cows and chickens, and many other things we see fit for humor. Jokes speak to that larger understanding—or, in some cases, to narrower groups or subcultures that nevertheless share a complete and common understanding. If they don't have that understanding, the only response will be: "I don't get it."

Put differently, a joke about Einstein only works if the person knows who Einstein was. (Note: Racist, sexist, and otherwise bigoted jokes use this in the worst way, playing off of not just shared understanding, but shared prejudices.) Context and familiarity matter, and they matter in the stories we tell, too—if people cannot relate, or cannot be *made* to relate to the characters or the setting or the situation, they'll be left scratching their heads and saying the same damn thing: "I don't get it." Every joke has its audience, and you tell it to *them*. Every story has its audience, too.

Third, rhythm matters when you're telling a joke. You can't just blurt it out. You need to bring the pauses, you have to speak in a relaxed way, you have to feel the comic timing. Stories rely on timing and rhythm. Just like a joke, you can't blurt out a story. You lead

---

[9] It's like cheap, hurried sex—it happens fast, and hopefully everyone has a good time.

in. You tease. You have to know the right time to take a breath and withhold the "punch line"—a punch line being a twist or a climax within the book. It's also true that you have to use the right words in establishing that rhythm. Big words and awkward sentences will kill a joke dead. And they can kill a story dead, too—you want clarity, you want a story that's as easy to slip into as the water in a warm tub.

Finally, a joke needs to do its job. A joke needs to be *funny*. It's great if it's also thought provoking or somehow profound, but those are not the uttermost functions of a joke. A joke that's not funny is not a joke. Now, a story is different in that a story doesn't need to be funny. That said, a *funny* story needs to be funny. A sad story needs to be sad. An adventure or a thriller needs to be exciting, and a scary story needs to be (drumroll, please) scary. Going in and telling a story means knowing what the story needs to do, and then tweaking it to do that. Comedians don't just blurt out hilarious shit all day. They aren't joke robots. They craft their humor. They practice their bits on stage and in front of people; they tweak the timing, they change the silences and applause breaks, they fidget with word choice. And a story is like that, too. Sure, it *sounds* natural and spontaneous, like you're just some erupting story volcano, but the truth is, stories are practiced entities. The best tales are those that have gone through countless drafts and countless retellings to get that precious bowl of bear porridge *just right*.

ON THE SUBJECT OF RHYTHM

The definitions of *rhythm* are abstract. A definition from Dictionary.com: "the pattern of recurrent strong and weak accents, vocalization and silence, and the distribution and combination of these elements in speech." Another definition (this one from Wikipedia): "movement marked by the regulated succession of strong and weak elements, or of opposite or different conditions."

These are useful in abstraction. But rhythm is *so damn important* to both writing and storytelling that intellectual abstraction can muddy the waters in terms of helping us understand what it is and why we need it. Instead, look to three things:

1. **HEARTBEATS.** A heartbeat is not an unchanging metronome. You have a pulse, and it goes up when you're excited and slows when you're calm.
2. **STORMS.** A storm is not merely the white noise susurrus of a steady rain, but rather a rise and fall in wind, a sudden flash of light and tumble of thunder, a heavy downpour slowed by a break in the maelstrom.
3. **SONGS.** A song is not just the same sound again and again: A song may start slow, then speed up, or vice versa; it may introduce new elements, new beats, new syncopations and sounds.

Rhythm for us must be this: not simply a repeated pattern, but a pattern that is predictable until it is not. In writing, rhythm works to give us a long sentence followed by a short one, a bunch of smaller words and then a big ol' fancy word. Rhythm in storytelling is about establishing trust and a lack of trust. It should feel as natural as our beating heart, or a stirring storm, or a song heard on the wind.

Stories are music and lightning and blood.

SPOKEN STORIES

Let's go back to my father. Like I said in the intro, he was a bona fide storyteller, even as he failed to really write or even read much. You know people like him. Maybe you *are* people like him. (You also know people who are the opposite of that. People who share boneless, clunky stories where nothing ever really happens, and you're thinking the whole time, *How do I get out of this? Could I just run away or do I need to puke in my hands first? Oh god please, someone text me or call me so I can say I have an emergency root canal I have to get to.*)

Damn Fine Story

I think I'm better now at telling stories in person than I used to be, though I'm much more comfortable telling stories using my brain and my fingers rather than having them spill out of the blabbering, blubbery bone-cave that lies hidden by my beard-nest,[10] and one of the ways I've improved is by observing people telling stories. I've tried to figure it out—how do they do that? What works?

The things that work for spoken stories also work for written ones, at least in part. Writing a book, a comic, a movie, whatever, they all have one thing in common: They are part of the cultural competition for dwindling time. They're here to entertain us and provoke us or, in a larger sense, to be *interesting*. All of us are like squirrels surrounded by nuts of various sizes, shapes, and flavors. We can, at any point, ditch the book we're reading to go watch Netflix, to check Twitter, to pick up a comic book, or to dick around on Facebook. We can play a video game, or nap, or wander into the woods like Sasquatch. We are *inundated* with options and opportunities to entertain and amuse ourselves.

If you're standing there, telling someone a story, they might not be rude enough to check their phones or suddenly turn heel and walk away from you because their Boredom Meter got filled up, but all the same, you're under pressure to entertain them. To be interesting. To have a point, any point, for fixing them with your gaze and sharing this tale.

A story told to someone standing in front of you demands some of the same panache as one that's written down. I sometimes like to make up stories for the Tiny Human, B-Dub, and *whistles* a five-year-old forms one of the most brutal, unforgiving audiences ever. You bore that kid, he'll make a poop noise with his mouth. A five-year-old has no such presuppositions of rudeness. He'll either give you a look like you're trying to teach math to a dachshund, or he'll just get up and walk away to go do something, anything, else.

---

[10] I know, I could just say "mouth," but god, what fun are words if we cannot stack them absurdly atop one another, pssh, c'mon.

You have to be interesting.

Consider the value in writing as if you need to entertain a five-year-old. You would have to keep the story moving. Ducking and feinting. Not just up and down, but left and right. Remember that earlier discussion about a story being less a mountain to climb and more a roller coaster to ride? *That*. You gotta be funny and inventive and quick on your feet. It's not enough to stand there and tell this kid about pirates who want a treasure. There have to be robots—or maybe butt-robots since, again, he's five. Just as he thinks he knows where the story is going, you have to *misdirect*, and then pull the rabbit out of your hat to surprise him.

That story from the introduction? Where my father smashed his pinky and then had to get it cut off? That story is still interesting enough if it's just, "I smashed my pinky and then the doctor cut it off." As a short, one-sentence tale, it flies. But when you've got a kept audience, and you want them rapt, the fact that the story has more going on is a value-add, right? It's in the gory details: *smashed in a log splitter, drove self to hospital, didn't want to pay the full price, went out to truck and got bolt cutters out of the back … and snippety-snip, like pruning a branch from a tree.*

It also *shows* you something about the character of my father without *telling* you. From the tale, you know he's tough. You know he's so bullheaded that he could probably win a head-butting contest with an angry moose. (Another story for another time is when my father wrestled a whitetail buck—a pet of ours named Rudy—to the ground, hog-tying it, even with two broken ribs from the deer's antlers.) You also know that my father is, in a word, *thrifty*, and that he distrusts the medical establishment to boot.

The details, the unspoken character components, the fact that the story is not a straight line to the end but has that vital twist (his reasonable thriftiness taken to unreasonable extremes when he cut off his own pinky rather than letting the doctor do it, an organic kink in the tale that lines up with the character that my father was)—that's what keeps people rapt.

It keeps them rapt when standing in front of you.

And it keeps them reading your book, or your comic, or watching your movie. So, when you're writing whatever story it is that you're writing, imagine that someone is standing there, listening. Imagine you have to keep them there, fixed to that point—this is a game, and you're the player, and the Scheherazadian goal is to keep them engaged. No, not engaged: *compelled.*

Interlude

THE SECOND RULE

The second rule is:

    Nobody puts Baby in the corner.

    Goddamnit. That … that doesn't sound right.

    Hold on, hold on.

    shuffles papers

    Ah. Oh! Ahem. Sorry, just need a moment to course correct, here.[1]

    The second rule is (drumroll, please):

    Character is everything.

    What I mean is this: A story can exist without a character, but only in the way that a human body can exist without a brain or a heart. You take those things away, the body remains a body, and it

---

[1] I fell asleep last night watching a Patrick Swayze movie marathon—as one is wont to do in these troubled times, for what greater balm for the soul is there than *Ghost* followed by *Dirty Dancing* followed by *Roadhouse*?—and obviously I made one of those notes where you're half-asleep and … well. We've all been there!

remains, by some definition, a human one. It just isn't alive. It has no purpose, it has no thought, and it certainly has no soul.

The reason we read stories is ultimately a selfish one. On the surface, we want to be entertained or enlightened, but deeper down, we're looking for a mirror. We want to see our stories reflected back at us. Changed, maybe. Tweaked in some way, or reflected in reverse. Possibly we're looking for a larger mirror—one to reflect not just our individual stories, but the story of who we are collectively, the story of where we are in place and time, a story to make sense of things.

At the heart of all of that? People. We connect to people. We build bridges to them. Empathy is king: We are putting ourselves in the stories of other people *and* relating their stories to our own experiences and ideas. People are everything.

Hell, *we* are people.

And people are characters.

(Now, to clarify, *characters* do not need to be people. Whether it's the toys in *Toy Story* or the piglet of *Babe*, characters need merely be characters, not human beings. You could write a book about a walking, talking, magical diaper, as long as you give the diaper an arc and some agency.[2])

A story without characters is a table without legs. It's still a place you can put your stuff, but it has no elevation. It is without its purpose.

We do this thing where we believe the story is greater than the character, but the reality is that the character or characters provide the reason for the story in the first place. We're like Yoda riding on Luke's back—we experience the story with and through the characters who are telling the tale or living that narrative.

And that feels like a pretty good segue into the next chapter, hm?

---

[2] Just don't elect the diaper president, please—we've had enough of that already.

Chapter Two

SOYLENT STORY: IT'S MADE OUT OF PEOPLE

I like to play video games.

I *especially* like to play video games where I am allowed to craft and create my very own character. When I was a writer and designer for pen-and-paper role-playing games,[1] my goal was to give the player as much control over his experience as possible. I wrote the games the way I wanted to play them: I wanted that control and rel-

---

[1] The kind like *Dungeons & Dragons*, in which you create and inhabit a character, describing your character's actions verbally to the other players present, and they do the same—and from this, a story begins to form.

ished it, and so I wanted the players of my games to have access to that same kind of experience.

When I get to create characters in a video game, I like to have the power to design how they look, what traits they have, where they come from. Even if all of that does not magically "auto-assemble" into a formal backstory, a backstory still manages to emerge in my head. Maybe it's just the storyteller in me, but I can't help but think, "My character is Elfblood McElvoy! He had a hard life, which explains his propensity for punching people and then picking their pockets. Also, he takes great delight in lying as a survival mechanism and he wears fancy purple pants[2] because I said so, that's why."

Then, even as I play, I might advance the character's story: "As Elfblood matures and grows more comfortable in planting roots, he decides it's time to buy a large, roomy house with a comfortable bed, because as a child he was forced to sleep inside a wicker basket. Also he was raised by angry bears, which is why he hates bears and kills a great many of them to keep their skins as rugs."

Or whatever. Point is, none of this is programmatically true in the game. The video game does not reinforce this backstory or even allow it to be codified. It's all in my head.

But that's okay.

What's interesting to me about this phenomenon is that I'm essentially creating backstory and stakes and conflict for the character that don't exist and that, at least in the context of the game itself, don't really matter. The game provides for me a narrative; just the same, I'm injecting my own narrative into it. Initially I wondered: *Is it just me?* Is it just because I'm a writer and a storyteller that I naturally drift toward invoking excess narrative? Am I that easily bored? Where are my pants?[3]

Ah, but then we had B-Dub, the Tiny Human.

---

[2] In real life I don't like to wear pants because Pants are a Tool of the Oppressor.
[3] See earlier footnote, re: pants.

I like to watch our Tiny Human play, and here's the thing you'll see when you watch kids play: They create characters and give those characters conflict. They don't do this because they are told. They do this because, to them, it's interesting. (And maybe, just maybe, because it helps them work through problems and discover solutions, as well as adjust to the reality that life is full of conflict. Which is perhaps one of the things that story gives us, too, even as adults.) B-Dub doesn't just have two action figures stand there and successfully make breakfast: They are besieged by conflict. Dragons! Robots! Dragobots! The Dragobots overcooked the eggs and now war comes to the Kitchen Kingdom! The toys talk and bicker. They fight and make friends. He infuses them with personality, and then puts them through the wringer. A story unfolds, chaotic and unrestrained. It's not the *best* story, no. It's not a story you'd want to put on paper—well, maybe, if you wanted to highlight the delightful absurdity of it. But it's got the hallmarks of story and character you want. The action figures—the characters—encounter conflict and sometimes change as a result, even if that change is that they simply *got dead*. The action figures affect one another. They have stories that begin and complete, though admittedly sometimes that completion is nothing more than AND THEN EVERYTHING EXPLODES as toys are flung about.[4]

To distill the point I'm making, the first thing my son does with his action figures is this: *He gives them a problem.*

So that's the first thing we need to talk about.

CHARACTERS ARE THEIR PROBLEMS

Writers are often exhorted to endure these somewhat cuckoopants "character creation exercises" to help them get to the heart of the

---

[4] Frankly, some of the best of us have gone with AND THEN EVERYTHING EXPLODES as the resolution of our plot. Stephen King is one of our greatest storytelling resources, and he ended the novel *IT* with AND THEN A GIANT SPIDER, I GUESS? Plus there was that thing with the preteen orgy, which is, uhhh. Yeah.

characters they're creating—we write imaginary job interviews, or we fictionalize the character's Twitter feed, or we instead explore a hundred different inane questions about them. (What's her favorite hair color? How long are her toes? If she were a piece of Ikea furniture, what piece of Ikea furniture would she be? A Billy Bookcase? A Klippan loveseat? Perhaps a Snorjn-pög Lingonberry-Flavored desk lamp?) It's not that it's *bad* to consider these things. It's just—are they really the best ways to get to the most vital aspects of the character? Does it really breathe meaningful life into them in a practical and critical way? Maybe! Maybe you find them useful. But for my mileage, I want as fast an understanding of what makes the character interesting on the page as possible, and that means encouraging you to consider the characters through the context of the story you hope to tell with them.

For me, the most efficient and compelling way to do that is to identify, right out of the gate, the character's problem.

And this is how the audience will see the character. The character *is* her problems. We remember her conflicts because that is who she is and why we are witnessing this particular segment of her life. Remember that thing I said (in the interlude on page 9!) about how a story is defined by the break in its status quo? So, too, is a character defined by her problems—and her problems represent exactly that breach of status quo I'm talking about.

Thinking about a character's primary problem isn't just a good way to figure out the character—it's the *best* way to conceive of that character's place in the story and the focus of the narrative.

Let's take John McClane, from *Die Hard*.[5]

It's tempting to think that John McClane's problem is Hans Gruber and his band of merry not-quite-terrorists. Thing is, that problem defines the plot, but it doesn't define John McClane. Meaning, it isn't the problem that puts *him* in the story.

---

[5] I know, I know, *that* movie, again? Buckle up, buttercup, we're going to see a lot more *Die Hard* in this book before it's over.

No, John McClane's problem is that he's separated from his wife, Holly. Right? That's his big issue. That's why he comes out to the West Coast, leaving New York City and his job as a cop there. It's why he joins a party full of people utterly unlike him. It's what gives him the motivation to survive, persist, and triumph. He has a family to win back.

Here you'll say, "Chuck, that sounds suspiciously like you've identified his motivation." And you're damn right. That is, in fact, his motivation. So why highlight it as his problem?

Motivation is often framed in a wifty, noncommittal way. A motivation might be, Fred wants to be rich. Or, Siobhan wants to do better in school. Or, perhaps, Chuck wants to stop pooping fire out of his butt.[6]

But those motivations are a little … *soft.* They're passive, not active. By framing them as problems, though, we put them front and center. We make them *present.* Problems are to be conquered within the story; motivations run the risk of continuing on forever, without solution, without end.

Buffy Summers has a problem: It's not vampires, but rather, it's that she wants to be a normal teen, and being the vampire slayer prevents this. That problem not only defines her character, it provides context for many of the episodes throughout *Buffy the Vampire Slayer.* If her problem were vampires, the *only* thing she'd be doing is running around sticking Mr. Pointy[7] into the chests of the undead. Which might be fun for about three episodes, and then we'd get bored. But that core problem of wanting to live a normal life and just be a teenager instead of a vampire-slaying freak show with an unshakable destiny—that's something that provides story fodder for years. Further, it's a problem we totally grok. We've all felt like freaks at times—or like society has expectations of us that we just can't escape.

---

[6] Damn you, Taco Bell!

[7] Mr. Pointy is the name she gives to the wooden stake she uses to slay vamps.

Luke Skywalker has something of the opposite problem: He's desperate to *escape* his normal life for a life of heroism.[8]

Luke Skywalker would do anything to be Luke Skywalker, Vampire Slayer, instead of Luke Skywalker, Womp Rat Bullseye-er. He's eager to escape the ugly, boring sand planet.[9] Tied into Luke's utter lack of adventure is that he's stuck with his stick-in-the-mud aunt and uncle—not his father, who apparently was an ace pilot and awesome dude back in the Clone Wars. Inevitably, Luke's no-good, dirt-farmer life is swept up in the cloak of an old chaotic Jedi named Obi-Wan, and, well, the saga unfolds from there. Further, Luke's initial "problem" disappears under the danger of the solution—as it turns out, sometimes the fix is worse than the problem. In story terms, Luke's problem changes and evolves as the Star Wars saga goes on. He solves one problem and replaces it with another, which keeps the story fresh and vital.

THE STORY IS THE SOLUTION

A character has a problem:

- My husband is trying to kill me.
- My child has been abducted.
- I am lost in the wilderness.
- Someone took the last jelly donut out of the box, and that was my jelly donut, goddamnit.

The character likely also has a solution:

- I will kill my husband before he kills me.
- I will take the law into my own hands to get my child back.

---

[8] We might think Luke's problem is "The Empire," but remember: At the start of *A New Hope*, he's literally planning on joining the Imperial Academy!

[9] Remember when a young Anakin Skywalker said that sand "gets everywhere"? I have to assume that even in his metal suit, Darth Vader is walking around with the grit of sand eternally irritating his nethers. Maybe that's why he's so mad.

- I will follow the river south in the hopes of escaping the wilderness and finding my way once more.
- I will hunt my nemesis across all the earth and all the stars until my foe is dead … or has at least returned to me the jelly donut he stole.

The character is the problem. And the solution is the story.

What I mean is this:

Between the character's problem and the character's solution *to* that problem lies the story. That is the character's *quest*. Implicit in the quest is a story. Ever watch the show *Dexter*, or read the book by Jeff Lindsay that it's based on? You have a character who is a serial killer, but the fact that Dexter can't stop being a serial killer is his problem. His father, Harry, gives Dexter a "code" that serves as *Harry's* solution to Dexter's problem—that code allows Dexter to kill, but only to kill bad people. Dexter's own solution to the problem of being a serial killer goes one step further, however:

He becomes a forensic blood spatter analyst for the Miami Police Department.

Dexter hides in plain sight. This affords him the opportunity to clean up his own murder scenes and steer attention away from him, and it grants him the chance to find new victims. But! It also causes Dexter a complication: By hiding in plain sight, he's also in scarily close proximity to the law, even as he breaks it. He is playing with fire, operating out of a department whose detectives are ultimately highly skilled at rooting out the truth.

All this translates to one larger idea:

The character creates the plot.

We have this idea of plot as a big, explosive thing. A galaxy in strife! A world in danger! Hidden treasure! Secret weapon! All of those things are very large, very plotty, yes.

They're also entirely external. They are *inorganic*.

Damn Fine Story

And yet, we often approach stories this way—and it's like trying to install a skeleton into the body after the child is born. It's not a *part* of the story. When storytellers have an exterior framework into which they then plug the characters, the characters operate as secondary, as afterthoughts. And the audience has no one to ground them in the story.

Characters are everything.

Characters drive the narrative.

Story is Soylent Green.[10] *It's made out of people.*

Plot is not some external thing. It is born directly of the people on the page.

Put differently, if story is architecture, then characters are the architects. Sometimes they're willing architects, other times quite unwitting. But they're architects just the same. Meaning, they build the story structure as they go, acting and talking and changing the narrative.

Everything can unfold naturally from that interstitial terrain where a character navigates the problems that she faces. That journey, that quest, has a core conflict baked right into it: The character wants a thing and must work to gain the thing. By drawing this as a problem in need of solving, you have "auto-magically" invoked conflict. Moreover, it's a personal conflict. Remember what I said about us seeing our stories inside the stories of the characters? They are how we relate. They are our vehicle to empathy.

Look at it this way: The core storyworld dynamic of the Empire versus the Rebellion in Star Wars is the big galactic conflict. But it

---

[10] *Soylent Green*: a 1973 film starring Charlton Heston, written by Stanley Greenberg, directed by Richard Fleischer. In it, the year is 2022, and climate change has ruined the world. Ahem. And in this dystopia, the world is fed rations by the Soylent Corporation, and the newest ration—which they claim is made of plankton—is called Soylent Green. Heston's detective, Frank Thorn, discovers that it's *not* plankton after all, and in the famous line of dialogue: "Soylent Green is people!" Oh, also, Soylent is a new meal replacement drink invented by Rob Rhinehart. And yes, that is a weird and creepy choice for the name of a meal replacement drink.

is meaningless without considering the roles of the characters both inside it and against it. That struggle between Evil Space Regime and the Plucky Band of Iconoclasts is the status quo. It's happening. It's ongoing. We begin the saga with that as the baseline for the events that are unfolding.

In terms of *Star Wars*, that baseline is then interrupted by the paths of our core characters, Leia, Luke, Han, and the like. It is the actions of these characters, in pursuit of solutions to their problems, that not only give us an entry point to the larger conflict, but also serve as the mechanism by which we discover and confront the greater galaxy. We don't get the story if Luke doesn't choose to pursue adventure off of Tatooine, if Leia doesn't work to pursue freedom for the galaxy, if Han doesn't work to be the debt-ridden scoundrel that he is. Without them, the *Star Wars* saga is just a boring-ass chess game. With them, it's something greater. With them, it's a *story*.

Ah, but, but, but—

A problem and a solution are not enough.

The quest itself is an uncomplicated tale. "I want the thing! Now I go get the thing. I have the thing! THE END."

Ugh. Dull.

Your job, as the storyteller, is to be as horrible as you can be. You are the Dungeon Master. You are the callous god. Your job is to place a labyrinth between the character and her solution. You must interrupt her quest at every turn with:

Complications.

RELATIONSHIP STATUS: IT'S COMPLICATED

To recap: John McClane's problem is that his family is recently broken up. His solution is that he's going to fly his ass out to the West

Coast and mingle with a party of coastal elites to try to rebuild the bridge to his wife.

Now, implicit in that is the central dramatic story. (Drama is the conflict between people. It auto-generates conflict and the story—admittedly, it tends to generate a more human one with far fewer, um, machine guns than we see in *Die Hard*.) McClane is a fish out of water in this context. He doesn't belong to this world; this world belongs to his wife. There's a power imbalance, and he's uncomfortable—and we see it in the opening act of the film when he has to ball up his toes and relax after a long flight.

But then the movie delivers its first real complication to that central drama:

Hans Gruber and his merry gang of not-quite-terrorists.

That complication is *itself* somewhat complicated: It's not *just* that terrorists show up, it's that John is separated from the party without much to help him. The guy doesn't even have a pair of *socks* on, since he was doing that thing with his toes on the carpet. Now, his discomfort at being with these people and in this corporate world suddenly pales in comparison to being separated from the group while trapped in a skyscraper as it's being locked down and taken over by violent thieves.

And that is only the first complication.

Every complication is a bend in the maze of the labyrinth that the writers put between McClane and the end of his quest. Every move the terrorists make against him is a complication. When the cops and the FBI show up and think *he's* part of Gruber's gang? Complication. When the media shows up to his house and involves his children—thus making Gruber realize that Holly is, in fact, John's wife? Not only is that a complication, but it raises the stakes of the relationship central to the drama (more on raising stakes on page 45). Each complication might lead him to a crisis point: a moment in the story where it seems that all is lost or that the way forward is impossible.

Every complication demands a response from the character it affects. In *Die Hard*, some of McClane's responses are proactive, with the character offering his own complications to the story. Example: When he throws a dead body out the window to get the attention of the patrolman below, *he's* the one complicating the story—both making it better for himself by recruiting an ally and worse in that he's just attracted a whole lot of attention to himself.

Ah, but these are not the only kind of complications.

INTERNAL COMPLICATIONS / LIMITATIONS

Complications aren't all surface. They're not all DOOM ROBOTS and ORC ATTACK and OH GOD, THE DOG JUST FARTED.[11] Besides, characters are not two-dimensional pieces of paper. They have their own architecture—and they have weaknesses in their design. Flaws in the code. Glitches in the Matrix. Exhaust ports on the Death Star.

Internal complications—or what I call "limitations," because they place limits on a character—add new bends and roundabouts and dead-ends to the maze. A limitation would be defined as a trait internal to the character that limits his ability to directly and correctly solve his own problem.

Buffy Summers—who, remember, wants to be a normal high school student (problem)—faces complications in pursuit of that problem in the form of, ohhh, just some vampires and demons and other assorted nastiness emerging from the Hell mouth that her entire town sits on. But she has her own limitations, too. For one, she's

---

[11] You think I'm joking, but those of you who have dogs know the room-clearing complication of canine gassiness. Especially if your dog is one of the more *snorfly* breeds—a flatulent pug is a violation of the Geneva Convention.

not very academic—it's not that she's not smart, but she doesn't really want to learn stuff, necessarily. She's resistant to it, and this makes dealing with her other complication—vampires and demons and Hell-mouth nasties—much harder. It also complicates her relationship with Giles, her Watcher.[12]

Han Solo has a limitation, too. If you say that his problem and solution are that he's a scoundrel with debts (problem), so he needs to take jobs that pay them off (solution), getting drawn into a galactic struggle between the Empire and the Rebel Alliance is of no use to him. His limitation, however, presses him further into service because, as it turns out:

Han Solo has a heart.

He's got this hard exterior made of sheer swagger and scoundrel snark, but the reality is, oops, Han Solo is actually a nice guy. Worse, he's a nice guy who is falling in love with Princess Leia, which adds one more complication/limitation to the pile—yet another bend in the maze. This hampers his ability to get the job (debts paid off) done.

Which is to say, it creates, complicates, and deepens his character.

And deepening his character also enriches the story.

Once again, we see how the two are inextricably bound.

THE STAKES ON THE TABLE

The stakes of the story are that which can be won, lost, or otherwise protected. What can be won arguably amounts to the character solving the problem. What would be lost is that the character has failed to solve the problem and must reap the harvest of his failure. (There's also an option to return everything to the status quo, which is to say the character does not precisely win or lose. It would be the

---

[12] If you don't know the series, a Watcher is the one who helps train and teach the Slayer.

equivalent of gambling your money and not coming out ahead, but not losing anything, either.)

A complication can raise the stakes, or change them.

Raised stakes mean that, in the gambling metaphor, there is now more to be won—and/or more to lose—than there was when the stakes were introduced.

The stakes at the outset of *Die Hard* are that John McClane can either fix his marriage or lose it. Then the first complication comes (oh shit, terrorist attack). When that happens, the stakes are raised—now, not only is his marriage in metaphorical danger, he and his wife are *literally* in mortal danger. Then, when Hans Gruber discovers who John's wife is—and the media also puts their children into play—the stakes are raised again. Another elevation of the stakes occurs when we learn that the terrorists are going to blow the whole building and that they have a plan that will result in the FBI killing the hostages. At each of these points, the conflict steps up. Things get worse. Much more is on the line.

Ah, but what happens when the stakes are *changed?*

The game becomes something else. The rules change. You thought you were playing Poker, but it's really Naked Battleship. And your opponent is an angry badger.

This is what happens to poor Luke Skywalker.[13] He goes along thinking that the path to adventure couldn't be clearer: He needs to take down the Evil Empire and its brutal enforcer, the Sith known as Darth Vader—coincidentally, also the same Darth Vader who, *gasp*, killed Luke's father, Anakin.

Of course, the truth is *way* screwier. Anakin (uh, spoiler warning?) never died. Instead, he was mauled by Obi-Wan Kenobi and burned with a whole lot of lava, and then shoved into the Death Metal tin can known as Darth Vader's scary-ass armor.

---

[13] Er, not the angry badger part.

Darth Vader *is* Luke's father.

Which does not merely elevate the stakes—it transforms them.

The battle Luke *thinks* he's fighting—as a newly minted rebel going up against an evil Empire and dad-killer Darth Vader—isn't the battle at all. Upon learning that his father is alive and is actually Darth Vader, the stakes change. It's no longer a galactic struggle. It's no longer a mission of justice or revenge. It's intimately personal, and, for Luke, totally conflicting. He's told he shouldn't face his father, but he wants to. He's told he isn't ready, but he's impetuous, eager, angry. He's *then* told that if he faces Vader, he's going to have to kill him—but he doesn't want to kill his own father. He learns, too, that Leia is his sister.[14]

The stakes change for him. He decides he's going to save his father, and he's going to turn that clanky old half-robot back to the light.

At the end battle, he throws away his lightsaber. He cedes the fight.

And *then* Vader probes his mind and learns about Leia, and once again, even so close to the end, the stakes change—*wham*, another sharp uptick like a spike in narrative blood pressure. Now Leia is in danger. And Luke fights harder than he's ever fought, almost falling into the yawning chasm that is (*dun dun dun*) the Dark Side to save her.

So much is happening in that last lightsaber battle in the Emperor's throne room. The entire galactic struggle is crystallized down to this pure moment between four people—Luke, his father, the Emperor, and, though she's not in the room, Leia. The fate of the galaxy is balanced on the fulcrum of individual characters. Not governments, not rebellions, not Empires. It's still about *people*.

And that's not unlike how things really are. We view history as this monolithic entity, this shifting tide of nations and city-states,

---

[14] He learns this after making out with her, so, uh, that's a thing.

of alliances and hostilities. But history comes down to people. History can change based on the whims of a president—or, in the right circumstances, a janitor.[15]

Point is, in your story, raising the stakes means simply adding to what can be won and what can be lost. *Changing* the stakes means transforming them: What was once a battle for someone's heart may become a battle for their life. What you thought was about money is really about independence. What was once a story of war and a battle of nations becomes instead about something internal—a struggle of a soldier against his own worst self. In The Hunger Games—literally a series about games—the "game" component changes, and Katniss's struggle ceases to be just about survival and becomes about something much larger—about overthrowing an autocratic regime. For her, the game has *literally* changed.

To change the stakes in your story, look for that hard shift.

PLOTTING VIA PEOPLE

If I'm doing my job right, then what you're starting to see here is a more organic way of plotting and telling a story. It is *character-driven storytelling*. A character has a problem and, in trying to solve it, faces external complications and internal limitations. She traverses the maze to accomplish her goals—and that journey through the maze *is* the story. THE END.

Ha ha ha! We did it! We figured it out. Together we learned to tell a story based on a singular character and—

Wait. What's that? Stop whispering. What are you saying?

A story is more than one character?

Oh. *Oh.*

So ...

How the hell does *that* work?

---

[15] I confess, I haven't thought that one through, but if you want an interesting story-writing exercise, write how a janitor changes the course of human history. Go on, do it, I'll wait. Are you done yet? GOD, YOU'RE SO SLOW, HURRY UP.

PARALLEL AND PERPENDICULAR CHARACTERS

We like to think and talk a great deal about protagonists and antagonists, and that's not a bad way to look at things, exactly. But it's vital to realize that those two terms are purely a matter of perspective.

What I mean is this:

Your protagonist is the agent of change in the story. The protagonist is the one with the primary problem in need of a solution. The protagonist may not *want* to be that agent of change—Bilbo doesn't, nor does Frodo, really, in Tolkien's work—but he becomes that agent of change, regardless, through the work.

Your antagonist is the opponent of the change sought by the protagonist, and quite possibly the agent of the dreaded status quo. The antagonist is part of the protagonist's problem, either as a complication to the solution or as a direct adversary seeking to countermand any efforts to fix the problem.

One is the hero.

The other is the villain.

(Neither is automatically the main character, so says the sidebar on page 53.)

The antagonist stands in the way of the protagonist being able to solve his problem. Very roughly put, the protagonist wants to go from *Point A* to *Point B*, but as he starts on his journey, the antagonist shows up and pummels him about the head, neck, and crotch with a Wiffle ball bat.

This breakdown can work for your story, especially if your story fits in a more traditional, trope-flavored mold. But greater nuance may be necessary.

Here's the problem with viewing every story and every character through the protagonist versus antagonist lens:

Every character believes himself the protagonist.

Not every character views himself as the *hero*, exactly, but at the same time, very few characters likely view themselves as the villains. Sure, we understand that Luke Skywalker is our Good Guy Protagonist and Darth Vader is our Bad Guy Antagonist, and, clearly, that works well enough.

Consider, though, that Darth Vader does not necessarily view himself as evil. If we take the story from *his* perspective, he is trying to protect the stability of the galaxy from a band of terrorists.[16]

In other words, Vader has his own problem, and his own solution *to* that problem. The Empire's status quo has been disrupted by these terrorists, since that bun-headed jerk, Princess Whatshername, sent the Death Star plans down in a droid so they could be intercepted by Obi-Jerk Kenobi. So Vader plans to retake the plans and quash the Rebellion—but *then* he's sidelined by some womp rat–killing teenager (complication!) who ends up a Jedi (complication!) and *oh crap* is also his son (complication, plus now he has an internal limitation given this sudden pull to the light)! The stakes are raised *and* changed! Vader shifts his own tactic—now it's not about shooting down that flyboy in the X-wing, but rather, urging him to the Dark Side so that the two of them can take on Palpatine together. And wait, there's a *sister*? And it's that jerk, *Princess Whatshername*? Complications, limitations, stakes changing, heads exploding!

Point being, Vader doesn't know he's evil. Sure, sure, there's that whole thing with blowing up an entire planet, but, to be fair, the rebels blow up an entire battle station. And while there's a difference there in the magnitude of civilian casualties, it's still worth looking at from different points of view.[17]

---

[16] We also learn that Vader may be trying to undermine The Emperor, Sheev Palpatine. Yes, that's right, the Emperor's name is Sheev. Which is the Star Wars version of Steve. Steve Palpatine. That wizened old goblin isn't so scary now.

[17] Say it with me *again*: "From a certain point of view."

And if you don't look at it through those alternate points of view, you again fall to the a-little-too-easy dichotomy of protagonist versus antagonist.

Characters are complex. They all view themselves as being right—and often righteous—in their pursuit of goals and solutions.

If we expect that characters are all fully formed, each with his or her own set of problems and solutions (and challenged in turn by complications and limitations, some shared, some unique to them), then we start to see an emergent storyworld full of individuals with competing desires. We don't see a single character moving in a single line—

We see dozens, even *hundreds* of character sharing the same narrative oxygen, each moving with and against each other.

It's the direction of that movement we should focus on.

In a web, some threads will connect at intersections and go in different directions. And some webs will hang alongside each other. So instead of protagonist versus antagonist, let's talk about parallel versus perpendicular.

Parallel means two lines traveling in the same direction, with the same amount of distance between them at any point on each line. (Think two lanes of a single highway traveling ever onward. Each lane goes in the same direction, but never do they converge.)

Perpendicular means one line traveling in one direction while another line intersects it. (Think one car traveling forward, another car T-boning it at an intersection.)

Luke and Leia are parallel characters. They both (roughly) share a single path, and they don't really deviate. They are on the same side of this war. Their precise problems and proposed solutions aren't always the same, but for the most part they are moving in the same direction.

John McClane and Al Powell (the cop he "recruits" by throwing a body on top of his cruiser) are also parallel. They're on the same team. They're both isolated in their own situations, so they make fast friends and allies.

Luke and Vader are *perpendicular*. Their quests are at odds with one another. So, too, are the quests of John McClane and Hans Gruber.

Now, the cool thing about a perpendicular relationship is that the shape it makes is a **t**. And when you turn the **t** on its side, *it's still a t*. Meaning, each character can be viewed, depending on the perspective—or the way you tilt the **t**—as being the one whose quest is interrupted. Vader interrupts Luke's quest, but Luke interrupts Vader's, too. McClane is trying to get back together with his wife, and Gruber is trying to rob a corporation, and both are essentially bonking heads like a couple of cantankerous elk.

Characters do not need to remain parallel or perpendicular to one another, either. Consider Spike or Angel in *Buffy*, or Prince Zuko in *Avatar: The Last Airbender*—these are characters who begin moving in one direction, then pivot. At different points, Spike and Angel both are antagonistic to, and allied with, Buffy. Zuko starts off as a zealous antagonist (a perpendicular force of intersection), but through the course of the show changes to move in parallel to Aang, the Avatar.[18]

The women of the show *Gilmore Girls* also operate in a way in which they are constantly moving in and out of parallel and perpendicular relationships with one another. This isn't to say any of them are openly antagonistic or serve as the "villains" of the series—to the contrary, a show like that is a very good example of why we need to think beyond protagonist/antagonist as our outer limits for

---

[18] Consider this your marching orders: If you haven't watched that show, get on it. Smart storytelling that lets the characters set the plot despite it being about prophecy and magic and a lot of the things storytellers use as plot crutches. Go watch it. Right now. I'll wait.

(I won't really wait, it's like, 60 episodes.)

what characters can be. Real life often includes people, even loved ones, who work for us *and* against us in equal measure. A parent is in many ways the perfect embodiment of this. It is my job as the father of a tiny human to a) help him become the best version of himself and b) stop him from jumping off our roof or eating gum off the floor at Walmart (or really any number of the things he wants to do daily that are not in his best interest). And isn't that a parent's trick? We even say it out loud:

"I'm doing what's best for you."

Thing is, what's *best* for the kid isn't always what the kid *wants*. And so the parent operates as both ally and enemy, in parallel *and* perpendicular ways. And sometimes we cross the line, thinking we're doing the best thing when we're not. Because we make mistakes. Just like kids make mistakes. This is life. This is story.

This is how people *are*.

PROTAGONIST VERSUS MAIN CHARACTER

Yes, Virginia, you can have a main character who is not your protagonist. A main character is the one who the narrative focuses on (or focuses through, via that character's perspective), whereas the protagonist is the agent of change.

Look no further than *Mad Max: Fury Road*. Mad Max is the main character, as it his name is on the film. Furiosa is the protagonist, for she is the agent of change and the one with the stakes on the table. Max may be the lens through which we view the film and its surroundings—we are granted, loosely, his perspective—but Furiosa is the one with the *quest*. And thus, she is the protagonist, while Max is merely the main character. Discuss.

THE IN-BETWEENERS

You might wonder—is there an in-between? Is there some remixed mash-up of both perpendicular and parallel, a directional symbol that is a little bit one, a little bit the other? In math, lines are either parallel, perpendicular, or *neither*; can that be true for characters? And what role would that serve?

Also, I realize I just said the phrase, "in math," which is a phrase that actually hurts me to say. As I typed it, my fingers started to itch, and my tongue swelled up to the size of a balloon. The right half of my brain tried to strangle and kill the left half. True story.

Still, *in math*,[19] when two lines are neither perpendicular nor parallel, they *still intersect*, but they don't travel along the same slope, and they don't form a ninety-degree angle. This speaks to two characters who are not *directly* competing, but who are also not uniformly allied—and yet, they are headed toward some manner of intersection—each path inevitably crossing the other's.

Example? Consider the Underwoods in *House of Cards* on Netflix. These two hypervenomous, narcissist characters, Frank and Claire, are married. They are moving ineluctably together, ostensibly toward the same goal of aggregating power for themselves. They help one another, but most likely only to help themselves. They may love each other, but that love is built on a kind of mutual appreciation of how utterly bloodthirsty they both are. And so, we see time and time again how they move toward conflict with each other, despite traveling in roughly the same direction.

If you want to find that kind of relationship in Star Wars, look no further than Vader and The Emperor (Palpatine[20]). Both serve the Empire. Both work together, with Vader in a loosely subservient position to Palpatine. The Emperor is subservient to no one, and the papery old goblin-wizard does whatever the hell he wants. As soon as Vader

---

[19] grrk! hnnn aaaugh it burns!

[20] Steve

makes the offer to Luke—"Join me and together we'll totally stab that old goblin-wizard in the face" (pretty sure that's an exact quote, by the way)—then we know that Vader and Palpatine are not necessarily on the same page. They will, as all Sith do, betray each other. The apprentice will slay the Master, or the Master will detect the coming betrayal and kill the apprentice to make room for a *new* apprentice (likely Luke). If you read the Star Wars novels and comics—nerd alert!—you will see even more signs of how troubled the Vader/Palpatine relationship is. They are moving together, but still toward conflict. Neither parallel nor perpendicular—even though each wants the other to *think* that their relationship is perfectly in parallel.

SUPPORTING CHARACTERS

I have a distaste for the term "supporting characters." It's not that it's a *bad* term, exactly, but it does call to mind a jockstrap or a bra—something created only to lift and support something else, that's purely architectural and not alive with that precious spark of life we assume characters should have.[21]

In the same way antagonists don't know they're supposed to be the Bad Guys, supporting characters don't know they're supporting characters. They are the protagonists and heroes of their own stories, and they don't know they're just punching in for a two-chapter appearance. They don't *know* that the book will only give them ten, maybe twenty total lines of dialogue. Off the page and beyond the screen, supporting characters have rich, complete, complicated lives. Or they don't, but they want those things for themselves—as we all do.

Supporting characters are just characters.

Which means you should treat them as you would Luke Skywalker or Hans Gruber. Figure out who they are. Look to the same

---

[21] If you have a jockstrap or bra that *is* alive with that precious spark of life, you should probably bathe more. And/or hire an exorcist. Remember, you need an old priest *and* a young priest.

elements that you'd give the main characters: What are their problems? How will they tackle those problems? What limitations and complications stand in their way? *Every* character is facing a maze. A labyrinth separates even the most meager character from the thing he most wants, from the end of his quest. We may not see it all, but like the peak of an iceberg we should still see *some* part of it poking out of the water.[22]

Who are some great supporting characters? From *Die Hard*, we've got Argyle, the limo driver who brings McClane to Nakatomi Plaza and gets trapped there when Gruber and the Gang take over the building. Argyle doesn't get a great deal of screen-time, but he *feels* like a complete character because he's given shape and dimension: We know he's got a girlfriend, we know he's lying to his boss, we can see him enjoying the high life in the limo in total ignorance (he raids the minibar and talks on the phone, using all the luxuries available to him). He also has a small character arc in that originally he seems like a bit of a screw-off (he's not your typical buttoned-up limousine chauffeur), but at the end he's called upon to play the hero. When he sees Theo, the hacker, prepping an ambulance for escape, Argyle slams the limo into it, thus foiling the bad guys' plans. The movie treats Argyle like he's got a complete life, and it even gives him a little climactic moment all his own.

Further, Argyle pulls double duty because not only does he have a life of his own, he also helps us understand McClane. Some characters work in parallel or perpendicular to one another, but others serve as *mirrors*—they reflect the characters with whom they interact. (Think Smithers and Mr. Burns in *The Simpsons*.) Argyle

---

[22] Consider the whale from *Hitchhiker's Guide to the Galaxy*, which appears in mid-air and, before plunging to its death, has enough time to experience a short journey of self-discovery and begin assigning names to things: "What's this thing suddenly coming towards me very fast? Very very fast. So big and flat and round, it needs a big wide sounding name like … ground! That's it! That's a good name—ground! I wonder if it will be friends with me?"

Damn Fine Story

challenges McClane, teases out information about him, his wife, his overall situation as a cop in New York City. He's a sounding board, a reflective surface, and an agitating element all in one.

The goal is to make them *seem* as complete and as interesting as you would any other character. They may have a limited role in this particular story, but we should feel like they have unseen, complicated lives off the screen or off the page.

As noted earlier:

Characters aren't just architecture—

They're *architects*.

And Argyle is a supporting element of this story, but he's also an architect in his own right. He supports McClane's story and helps us to understand it, but he gets beats that are his alone, and he actively affects the story. (We talk more about beats as a narrative measurement on page 86 of this book.)

Want an even *better* example of a character who functions as a mirror?

Wheezy the penguin, from *Toy Story 2*.

If you don't know Wheezy, he's a squeaky toy penguin that belongs to the human boy, Andy, along with the panoply of other living playthings that form the cast of characters. Wheezy, though, he's an *old* toy. The squeaker has gone out of him. And now he, well, *wheezes*.

Wheezy reflects the problem that the main character, Woody, has throughout the film: Woody's afraid of being an old toy put up on the highest shelf and forgotten—

Just like Wheezy.

See, Andy has forgotten his old toy. The high shelf is a special Hell for those toys, where they go into effective exile.[23] Woody gets put up on that shelf when he is himself busted. It's up there that he

---

[23] The *Toy Story* movies are pretty awesome, and they *seem* light and fluffy, but holy crap, do they get dark sometimes. The ending of *Toy Story 3* is one of the most existentially bleak climaxes I have ever seen on film. I still have flashbacks.

meets the raspy toy penguin—a penguin with some history, a character who has clearly had a long life that he fears is effectively near his end. It's the glimpse of the iceberg's peak: We don't see the details of Wheezy's history, but we know it's there.

Wheezy is an avatar representing the theme of the film: that we all risk being forgotten. Wheezy is also an agent of foreshadowing, reminding Woody and the other toys of their own effective mortality.[24]

Wheezy, though, has an arc, because eventually a happy ending is in store for him—he has his squeaker and his Robert Goulet–provided voice restored. And the other toys earn the same happy ending: None are forgotten, all are beloved, and they can go back to forgetting their mortality (until the next movie, that is).

THREE TIERS AND THREE BEATS

Characters fall into three arbitrary, I-just-made-these-up-to-help-you-determine-their-importance-in-the-story, tiers:

1. **ESSENTIAL CHARACTERS.** These are characters without whom the story really doesn't exist. In *Die Hard*, it's John McClane, it's Holly, it's Hans Gruber. But it's also a so-called "supporting" character Sergeant Al Powell, whose presence is vital because he's McClane's single ally in the film—he's a desk jockey cop who shows up and serves as John's only connection to the outside world. Powell is a tent pole. Without him, the whole thing falls down.
2. **USEFUL, BUT NONESSENTIAL.** Argyle in *Die Hard* is useful, though you could write that movie without him. These characters push on the plot and help generate (or resolve) both drama and conflict while nevertheless not being critical components to the overall narrative.

---

[24] Like I said: grim.

3. **FUNCTIONAL ONLY.** Gruber has a few guys in his crew that are there just as obstacles to be overcome—they have little-to-no inner life; they offer us nothing in terms of who they are or what they want. They may affect the story, but they do so in a fairly linear, singular way. They are, in the words of culinary wizard Alton Brown (see next sidebar), single-serving "unitaskers."

Now, even the most meager, walk-on characters should be given at least three beats (a beat is a form of narrative measurement that we'll talk about in the next chapter). It amounts to giving them three moments to exist, but ideally to do something that emblemizes the character or furthers the plot.

In *Die Hard*, the mighty Al Leong plays a minor character— a terrorist, Uli. He has very little to do in the script except, you know, to be a gun-for-hire. Even still, he has little moments that add up:

1. He is among the terrorists who take the thirtieth floor of Nakatomi Plaza hostage.
2. In the middle of a shoot-out, Uli stops long enough to eat some candy bars he found in a food stand. (Which is amazing, by the way. If I'm ever in a shoot-out with the LAPD SWAT, I hope to be awesome enough to steal and eat a Snickers bar as bullets zip past my head.)
3. Later, he helps plant the C4—and is then shot by John and blown up by the explosives he planted.

Again, it's not much. But it's just enough to give him the glimmer of a personality, to allow him to appear more than just a houseplant.[25]

---

[25] That's a pretty good test, by the way. If your character can be replaced by a houseplant or a sexy lamp without any significant change to the story, you either need to cut the character or give them more to do inside the narrative.

UNITASKERS VERSUS MULTITASKERS

Alton Brown identifies certain appliances or gadgets in your kitchen that have one narrow, niche purpose—like, say, a garlic press, or maybe a banana slicer. It's not that they don't do their job—it's that they take up space when you could use another object to perform the task competently. You don't need a banana slicer because you can use, oh, I dunno, a *knife*. A knife is a simple, elegant multitasker. It does whatever you need it to. You can cut bananas. You can slice garlic or use the flat of the blade to smash the clove. You can use the knife to stab whoever tries to steal your sandwich.[26]

In fiction, we also have unitaskers and multitaskers, though they are a little harder to see—sometimes, we refer to unitaskers as "darlings,"[27] meaning elements inserted by the author that serve little to no purpose except to please the author. A character you put into a story who has no connection to the rest of the story is, at best, a unitasker. A plot point that exists just because it seems cool is, again, a unitasker. It serves only itself.

Narrative multitaskers, though … ahh, there's some good stuff. A character who pushes on the plot, who ably represents the theme, and who isn't just a precious peacock there to preen and look pretty—*that's* what we're looking for. Elements should be able to do more than one thing. To go back to the architecture metaphor, a unitasker is nothing more than a model home—it has no function except its own display. You can't live in it, there's no electricity, no running water. A real house becomes a home by dint of its many functions. Your story can't just be a model home. And the elements within have to be more than that. They have to be more than just some single-use, bullshit object lost in a kitchen junk drawer. Each element must be an essential tool with many functions.

Begone, narrative banana slicers.

For our stories, we seek only sharp, shiny knives.

---

[26] I am not condoning stabbing anyone. But also if you try to steal my sandwich I will legit stab you. Ha ha ha, I'm just kidding. (I'm not kidding.)

[27] Found in the common writing advice chestnut, "kill your darlings," also known as, "stab those who would steal your delicious sandwiches."

BEHOLD: THE ARC

So wait, what the hell is a "character arc?" Isn't it that boat, where Noah put two of every animal except the unicorns because apparently Noah, that jerk, had a thing against unicorns? (Answer: No, that's the Ark.) Is it a piece of architecture? (Answer: No, except maybe yes if you count architecture in the narrative sense.) The arc is the shape of a character's development through the story. And key to that idea of "development" is also one of transformation—the best characters end a story *changed*. They leave the story a somewhat different character from when they entered it.

Sometimes the assumption is that the arc is connected to plot— it charts literal events crucial to the character, or it charts the decisions and actions made by the character—but that's not precisely right. Eschew plot. Think about story. Think about the emotional makeup of the story. Think about who that character is and what she or he represents.

An arc can be pretty granular, with subtle shifts in a character from chapter to chapter. But for our mileage, I like to at least give a character three tent pole transitions that mark her journey through the story.

Who is she when the story begins?

Who is she in the middle of the tale?

And who is she when the curtains finally close and the story ends?

Some of this can be pretty surface, right? Luke Skywalker in *A New Hope* goes from *farm boy, hungry for adventure* to *not-quite-getting-this-Jedi-thing* to *rebel pilot who trusts in the Force and saves the day.* Those descriptions chart his journey in short, easy-to-grok beats. Note, too, that we've tied in his problem here: that he wants to be free of Sandy Crack Junction and have some proper fun out in the larger galaxy. More to the point, he wants to be like his father.

The arc factors in the problem and charts the character's beats in dealing with it.

His arc gets more interesting when you factor in all three of the Original Saga movies, right? He goes through even more stages:

1. I'm going to be like my father and be a Jedi!
2. I'm going to get revenge for my father's death and stop Darth Vader and his oppressive Empire.
3. Wait, whoa, what? Darth Vader *is* my father?
4. Change of plans: I'm going to save my father's soul.

That charts a huge emotional turn for Luke. He goes from being *eager and naive* to *impetuous and angry* to, finally, *self-actualized and incorruptible*.

Or, in shorter beats:

He goes from *impatient* to *selfish* to *selfless*. And, along the way, he also struggles with his own faith in the Force—and his own faith in himself.

It's important to realize that a character's arc is not set in stone, nor is it artificially or externally driven. The changes in a character—the transitional movement in the arc—aren't like a clock where the tick-tock is automatic. The character learns things, sees things, and does things—all of which change who the character is. These gradual transformations don't happen because the story needs them to happen or because some PLOT BEAT WORKSHEET tells you that you're Half-Past a Change-O'-Heart. Yes, sure, of course, *you* might as the storyteller be aware that you have to get the character to that transformation, to that change-o'-heart. But it's *your* job to convince us of the reality of the change, and one of the ways you do that is by building it into the story, by making the journey there an organic one driven by the character and those around her. It's not external, not artificial.

YIPPEE-KI-YAY: OR, HOW EVERY MOMENT CAN SPEAK TO STORY AND CHARACTER

In *Die Hard*, when John McClane and Hans Gruber first speak—which is the pivotal, vital moment where your Hero and your Villain first encounter one another, dun dun dun—they have a short exchange. It goes like this:

> **HANS GRUBER:** Mr. Mystery Guest? Are you still there?
>
> **JOHN MCCLANE:** Yeah, I'm still here. Unless you wanna open the front door for me.
>
> **HANS GRUBER:** Uh, no, I'm afraid not. But, you have me at a loss. You know my name but who are you? Just another American who saw too many movies as a child? Another orphan of a bankrupt culture who thinks he's John Wayne? Rambo? Marshal Dillon?
>
> **JOHN MCCLANE:** Was always kinda partial to Roy Rogers actually. I really like those sequined shirts.
>
> **HANS GRUBER:** Do you really think you have a chance against us, Mr. Cowboy?
>
> **JOHN MCCLANE:** Yippee-ki-yay, motherfucker.

Let us speak now about the amazing amazingness of *yippee-ki-yay, motherfucker*.

In a lot of action movies—really, in a lot of movies, TV shows, books, and comics—the hero says some cool shit just to say some cool shit. It's part of the trope: whip-crack smart-ass hero protagonist who is funny and entertaining and edgy, tormenting the villain with his quick wit. (Sometimes it's the villain who gets the quips, and sometimes the hero and villain try to out-quip one another.) It's part of the package simply because it's part of the package. Tropes are like that, sometimes, just a lazy reiteration of a narrative element whose presence is justified by all the other times people have used this exact lazy reiteration.

Ah, but! With John McClane, the quip isn't *just* a quip.

It tells us about his character, and it grows organically out of a conversation. He isn't just saying cool shit to say cool shit. He's matching wits with Gruber, and we're learning that McClane sees himself as a classic American cowboy in this situation. So classic that he's not like John Wayne, but rather like someone farther back, back in an era of sequined shirts and a horse named Trigger. McClane is telling Gruber—and us!—that he's one of the good guys, that he's not part of some "bankrupt culture"; he's an old classic, the kind they don't make anymore.

Gruber snidely asks him if he thinks he'll win, then he calls him "Mr. Cowboy." McClane's response is, of course:

Yippee-ki-yay, motherfucker.

The *yippee-ki-yay* component speaks to how he sees himself: as a hero, part of a legacy of old cowboys. He's using a word that echoes back in part to Roy Rogers, Gene Autry, Bing Crosby. It's almost an aspirational thing to say, and it's immediately one he corrupts with the addition of that final word: "motherfucker."[28] Because McClane *isn't* an old-timey cowboy, strumming his guitar around the fire. He's a grime-streaked New York City cop, trapped in a Los Angeles skyscraper like a rat in a maze—he's not the kind to saunter in on a horse, but the kind to kick a dead body out of a window to catch the attention of a retreating police officer. And yet, *despite* that, he's still a hero, still the good guy.

He's the cowboy, he's the good guy—but in his own blood-soaked, mercenary, get-shit-done way. It's a modern retrofit of a classic mode. McClane is a hero for us, of that time.

Say it with me, now:

Yippee-ki-yay, motherfucker.

That line grows naturally out of a conversation *and* it reflects who McClane is. It's not just some clever pun meant to indicate the smartness of the hero. It's a short phrase, but provides us a deeper dive.

---

[28] See, I told you this book had naughty language. If it bothers you, for an additional five bucks I will go through your book by hand and change all instances of the word "motherfucker" to "monkeyflinger."

It is bound to the character because it comes out of the character.

The arc is like this: Our characters do not transform because we the writers demand they do. They transform because we build that into them, because we give them a journey that is difficult, that challenges them, and that changes them organically. Further, it changes them gradually, too: If a character changes too dramatically, the audience will suffer the whiplash of disbelief. It's our job as storytellers to *earn* their belief, to gain their trust, and to prove it with every page.

That emotional journey has to feel justified.

Furthermore ...

WE NEED TO UNDERSTAND THE EMOTIONAL JOURNEY

Simple is better. Clarity is king. It's true for almost all aspects of your story.

In *this* context, it means that you should keep the emotional journey of the character—and, really, the problem that inspires this journey—simple to understand.

Like I said in the last chapter, we often look to others' stories to find our own story hidden within. More to the point, we're seeking to build an empathic bridge with the characters: We want to go along for the ride. Further, we want the story to give us something we recognize in ourselves or in our own lives (even if "what we see" is really just an illusion or otherwise lines up with the aspirations of our own warped, circus-mirror self-image). We need the audience to relate to the characters and to the story those characters help to tell.

If we give the characters an emotional throughline—a throughline being the invisible rope we use to pull ourselves through the narrative—that is unfamiliar to most, then we have given the audience little opportunity to connect to the characters and that story. And note, I don't say *plot*. It's fine to have some, or even many, plot elements in play that people don't actively understand. I've never tried to explode a moon-size battle station or save a skyscraper from a gaggle of mostly German terrorists. But I *have* keenly felt Luke's problem of being trapped in a nowhere town, and his problem of confronting a father who seems to be an enemy. I totally grok John McClane's problem of being in a relationship in which two people seem to be going in different directions and the hell you might go through trying to mend that widening gap. The rest of it—Wookiees and explosions and gunplay—is all just the cool stuff you use to frame the core emotional journey.

We all understand the fundamentals: love, hate, revenge, grief. We know what it's like to have loved ones die, to have relationships fracture and end, to lose things we adore. We know pain. We know what it is to be hurt, emotionally and/or physically. We may not know the precise version you're putting on display in the story, but we can extrapolate. The audience is eager to do work. We don't need everything fed to us. We'll dig the hole.

You just have to give us a shovel.

We need to relate. It's one of the reasons that, to my mind, viewers connected more easily to the original three films of the Star Wars series (Episodes IV, V, and VI) than the later prequels—the prequels present characters rooted to Byzantine politics and trade agreements and zzzz *snore* *whoa*, hey sorry, fell asleep there for a minute. Did I drool? I probably drooled. Here, hold on, I'll just clean that up.

The prequels *try* to give us human stories, what with Anakin's fear of losing Padmé and his eventual jealousy over Obi-Wan, both of which start to creep up in Episode II, but by then it's too late. Anakin ultimately becomes the antagonist (meaning he turns perpendicular, working against all those around him), so it becomes even *harder* to relate—because while it gave us *some* emotional throughlines we understand, Anakin's *responses* to those emotional beats are not ones to which we relate. He throws tantrums and acts out and embraces the Dark Side, and (though we've probably all been there) the writing doesn't convincingly sell that transition as something we can be sympathetic or even empathetic about. He's mostly just a petulant monster at that point.

And as for the rest of the prequel characters? Their concerns and emotions are mostly academic—elite and haughty. We don't connect easily to abstract concerns. All the mechanisms of plot, all the flywheels flipping and gears turning, don't mean squat to us if we aren't grounded in *feelings we understand*. Obi-Wan comes closest in that he loses a mentor early on and is forced into being a teacher and proxy parent when he wasn't ready to be one, but no other character comes closer than arm's length because their worries are all about the Big Story.

The problem is, though, it's always the *small* story that matters. Even the biggest story must have a smaller, more human story nested at the center. (For more on that, please see the interlude on page 79.)

Like nougat.

DELICIOUS, NARRATIVE NOUGAT.

God, now I'm hungry for a candy bar. See what you've done? But at least we can all relate to that, because who amongst us does not occasionally let our sweet tooth have a say? Let's indulge!

shamelessly eats a candy bar while staring at you

and another

and twelve more while never once breaking eye contact

What was I saying? Right.

The small story is more important than the big story. In *Saving Private Ryan*, the war is a vital and necessary component to that story, but *it isn't the story*. It provides the plot, yes. It creates context, true. But the *story* is about the characters: the soldiers moving through the battle, trying to find one other wayward soldier who has survived when his literal brothers have not. And the soldiers we travel with, these characters, are men—boys, practically—who just want to go home, but aren't allowed to because they first have to help this *other* soldier go home. They're in the middle of something they can't control. They have only each other.

That's fundamental, ground-level humanity right there. We don't just understand it intellectually. We feel it right here, in our chests. It allows us to tether ourselves to the characters—so when they're in danger, *we're* in danger. When they're triumphant, *we're* triumphant. The act of storytelling is in part about creating those tendrils of empathy that bind us to the story. The act of storytelling is, weirdly enough, one where we hurt or help the characters in order to affect *you*, the audience. We want you to cry. We want you to cheer.

Really, we're monsters.

(And it's so much fun.)

Point being this: If we can't understand the character? If we don't see ourselves or something recognizable glinting back at us in their eyes? If there's no glimpse of humanity? We will put the book down or turn off the movie, because our options for Other Things To Do is not in short supply. We will fuck right off to the next book, the next show, or some app on our phones, or maybe we'll just eat a candy bar and take a nap.

A RESPONSE BEFITTING THE PROBLEM

Not only does the emotional journey (the quest resulting from confronting the problem) need to be something we grok, but we also need to respect and understand the response of the character.

To reiterate, when a character has a problem, that character also intends to solve that problem. And the journey from problem to solution is where we find the roots of our story and the events of our plot.

Just as the problem needs to be one we understand, so too does the solution need to be simple, clear, and relatable. John McClane's problem is his broken family, so his response is in no way alien or bizarre: He goes out to see his family and try to mend the damage. Now, that gets a lot more complicated when Gruber and the Gang shows up, but it's not mysterious. It's not a solution that leaves us scratching our heads. The motivation is clear, and the solution that comes out of that motivation is straightforward.

To go back to the Star Wars prequels, those films give Anakin an understandable, relatable problem: He's trapped in the throes of forbidden love and is slowly driven mad by his recognition of mortality—first witnessing the death of his mother, then becoming obsessed with a fear of Padmé dying, too. From there grow the limitations of his character: jealousy, anger, fear. Where the prequel trilogy starts to fall down a little is when Anakin's response to his problem is muddy and inconsistent. He becomes afraid of losing Padmé, even though the story offers us little evidence for why this fear grows so strong. And when his response to that fear is, WELP, GUESS I'LL FALL TO THE DARK SIDE, KILL SOME JEDI, MURDER SOME CHILDREN, MAYBE FORCE-CHOKE THAT LADY I LOVE, THEN ATTACK MY BEST FRIEND ON A LAVA PLANET, he gets further and further away from being a character we understand. Even as a villain, his journey seems strained and designed only to force[29] the plot to happen.[30]

Worse, Vader's eventual redemption at the end of *Return of the Jedi* is complicated by the events at the end of *Revenge of the Sith*. Luke believes that there is still good in his father, and Obi-Wan tells Luke as much—so we, the audience, believe that. But what we later *see* in the prequels is an impetuous, vengeful teenager whose decision to murder children and abuse the mother of his own future chil-

---

[29] Pun not originally intended, but it's too late now, damnit.

[30] This is also one of the tricky bits about prequels: In a prequel, the future is already written, and so the characters in a prequel are slaves to a plot that must find that future. The plot cannot organically grow and change from their actions because the stars are writ, destiny is sealed, the deal is done.

dren is so far outside of our relatable experience that it strains, or even breaks, our belief that he is someone worthy of redemption. It becomes less credible that Anakin has any good in him at all because his decisions are not ones we comprehend. If Anakin had jealously attacked Obi-Wan but obsessively sought to protect Padmé—oh, and if he hadn't just killed a bunch of kids—we might be able to get on board with him being a good person who was led astray. But the atrocities he commits, especially without due cause for his actions, are signs that he wasn't led astray—he was *always* astray.

THE UNCHANGING CHARACTER

An arc is predicated on a character changing—she transforms throughout the story, exiting a different person from when she entered.

Ah, *but*. There exists a type of character—often one cast in a more "heroic" mode—who never really changes. In most stories, a character engages with the world, it engages with her in return, and both come out different. Sometimes subtly, sometimes apocalyptically. But in certain stories, heroic characters push on the world—and it never pushes on them in turn.

This is where you have *static* characters instead of *dynamic* ones. In the original *Ghostbusters*, the four protagonists don't change much at all during the course of the film—they go through plot stuff, they bust ghosts and say funny things and save the whole damn city, but the characters who saunter out as heroes at the end aren't much different from when we met them at the beginning. Their *plot* is different. They have new roles—from shlubs to saviors, from zeroes to heroes—but that hasn't changed them in an organic, emotional way. Similarly, Indiana Jones as a character changes from film to film, but within each given film there's not a lot of movement for him emotionally. It's different in Star Wars—there, the characters are more dynamic. We talked about Luke already, but Han Solo goes from scoundrel to soldier; Leia's journey is less overt, but she goes from resisting love to embracing it, her veneer as a haughty princess cracked by the charm and smarm of the scoundrel, Solo. (That said, her badass-ery and her heroism is not diminished by any of this.)

Point is, it's totally okay to have a character not change throughout a story—depending on the *type* of story. It's certainly common in comic books and TV shows, where the writers don't really know how many episodes or issues they have to work with—could be five, could be five hundred. Which means you have no real ending to contend with, no shape, no dimension, and it's hard to plan for a character changing if that character might be, for all intents and purposes, eternal. (It has been said of television, and I'll say it's also true of long-running comic series, that the stories are "all middle.") Batman is still Batman decades later. He's changed somewhat with the times, but overall, his story remains the same, and his character exists within a spectrum of a degree. Superman, still Superman. Gregory House in the series *House, M.D.* remains the same cantankerous, ego-fed jerk-off that he was at the beginning.

What's interesting is that, sometimes, the static nature of a character is the *point* of the character. Tony Soprano and Don Draper (of *Sopranos* and *Mad Men*, respectively) are two characters who *try* to change. They are desperate to be different men with different lives. But at the conclusions of the shows' final seasons, the arc of each character was revealed to be not so much a bending rainbow as an ouroboros—a snake biting its own damn tail.

Still, when in doubt, give your characters an arc. Find a change for them, even a subtle one, even if the attempt to change reveals that they cannot. Consider how James Bond these days is seeing some emotional wiggle room (particularly in *Casino Royale*), which creates a deeper character—not a shallow trope-painted automaton marching bulletproof through the plot, but a three-dimensional *person* who has wants, fears, a problem, a quest. Creating characters with some transition, some transformation, makes them interesting—it breaks the status quo and gives us a reason to care.

And speaking of reasons to care …

SAVING THE CAT, ONE CHARACTER AT A TIME

There exists a popular book on writing screenplays called *Save the Cat!* by the late Blake Snyder. It's a damn fine book to help tuck your brain-meat into the conceptual sandwich that is "structure in film." It takes your expected three-act structure (which we'll talk about more starting on page 88) and makes it more granular, offering a more detailed view of those peaks and valleys that you need to hit in the screenplay. One of those peaks is a moment that earns the book its name: At some point in a film, the protagonist needs to perform a "save the cat" act—which is not literally to say every character in every film needs to actually perform feline rescue operations, but rather, that every character needs to give us at bare minimum a single moment where they are heroic. They do something noble or good to prove to us why we're with them on this journey.

As a piece of advice, it's not bad.

But I don't know that it's quite right, either.

Here's what I propose, instead:

I often refer to a "give-a-fuck" factor when writing characters—meaning, we need reasons to care. Having them metaphorically save a cat is one *possible* way to do that, especially if their arc is heroic. But we have another way, and it connects to what I've just been talking about:

Give them *relatable* moments. And not just one, either. As many as you can give us within the appropriate context of the work. A relatable moment occurs when a character connects with humanity in common ways, demonstrating shared experience.

It's like this: John McClane is tense from a plane flight, so another passenger has him do the "ball up your toes and push them into the carpet" ritual. That's very human. And a guy like McClane *needs* that humanity. He needs to be grounded, because otherwise he's just Snarky Supercop. But he smokes, he gets emotional, he makes bad decisions—and these are all very human things. We want him to feel like he belongs in his world, but also that he belongs in ours. In the movie *John Wick*, the titular assassin offers up a number of small human moments during the first act: waking up to an alarm, loving his new puppy, replaying a video of his deceased wife. None of these moments are related to his BADASS ASSASSIN life—they're moments related to regular life. To *life*-life. The kind we all have and can understand. Buffy Summers gets a lot of these moments as a kid in high school, and so does Peter Parker outside of being Spider-Man. Why we care for these characters—the *give-a-fuck* factor—isn't just about their heroism, big or small. It's about how human they are, and how that helps us to understand them.

ANAGNORISIS, PERIPETEIA, CATASTROPHE, AND OTHER ARISTOTELIAN SHENANIGANS

If you care to glance at Aristotle's theory of tragedy, or you really want a few words that will get you some big wins in Scrabble, I give you: anagnorisis, peripeteia, and catastrophe. My definitions here are very limited, but might give you a new way to look at both a character and her journey through a story:

Anagnorisis is a discovery made by a character.

Peripeteia is a dramatic change (positive or negative) in the story.

Catastrophe is the final resolution of the interplay between the above two forces within a story.

Anagnorisis and peripeteia are forces of order and chaos, respectively, that tumble around and around like a pair of hedgehogs fighting in a washing machine. So a character makes a discovery, which leads to a change, and/or a change leads to a discovery. And inevitably these two forces ratchet up and up until the conclusion—or catastrophe. You can think of this interplay between anagnorisis and peripeteia as encompassing the whole story, or perhaps see a story as a series of catastrophes (climaxes and resolutions) creating greater and worse conflicts until the end. Arguably, the former has a more typically mythic storytelling structure. *A New Hope* sees the dread order of the Empire battle the noble chaos of the Rebellion—and the Dark Side battles the Light, as well—leading to the rather large catastrophic conclusion of the Death Star going all explodey.

A television show, however, might be more useful to view through the lens of the battle of order and chaos resolving in a series of episodic catastrophes and conclusions—one after the other, act to act, episode to episode.

CHARACTER AGENCY IS EVERYTHING

If you've read this chapter on character and you've faded in and out, I don't blame you. It's okay. You, like some of my readers, have read the chapter and fugued out, waking up in an unearthed coffin somewhere west of I-95 in Maryland. You have no pants and your wallet is gone. It's okay. This happens *all the time*. It's a normal side effect of reading my books.[31]

Just the same, I want you to leave this chapter with a *point*, with something *actionable*. So if you exit this section learning nothing else, I want you to come away with this:

The greatest thing you can do for your characters and their story is to give the characters *agency*.

Agency does not mean they are literal members of, like, the CIA or the NSA. It doesn't mean they belong to some character guild or union where they'll demand a certain appearance ratio in your sto-

---

[31] Thank you for the wallet. I burned the pants.

ry. ("If these characters don't get at least ten lines of dialogue and a proper arc, then we'll see you on the picket line, Mister or Missus Fancy-Pants Writer-Person.")

No, character agency is this: a demonstration of the character's ability to make decisions and affect the story. This character has motivations all her own. She is active more than she is reactive. She pushes on the plot more than the plot pushes on her. Even better, the plot exists as a direct result of the character's actions.

Let's break that down a little.

- **MAKE DECISIONS AND AFFECT THE STORY.** This means that when the character says, "I need to go to my mother's house," the story follows her there. It means that when she says, "I am at my mother's house and I've decided that she needs to go into a nursing home," that becomes the story, or at least one part of it. The story isn't a train heading down the tracks and the character isn't a goat that the train is going to run over. The character *is* the train—or, better yet, the character is a helicopter or an ornithopter or a giant-ass bird who chooses her own three-dimensional pathway through the world. When her wings beat, currents are stirred and the world changes.[32]

- **THE CHARACTER HAS MOTIVATIONS.** At the fore of this, we said that characters have problems and they want to solve those problems. That's the motivation. They have a drive to do something—they want to gain something, they want to be rid of something, they want to love a person or find a widget. This is their quest, and they are on it not because the plot wants them to be, not because you the storyteller need them to be, but rather because they have the motivation to traverse the labyrinth.

- **ACTIVE VERSUS REACTIVE/PUSHING ON PLOT MORE THAN IT PUSHES ON HER.** Characters are not paper boats in a stream going

---

[32] Translation: Characters will do shit and say shit, and when that happens, it matters. It changes the world in ways both small and epic.

where the story takes them. The story goes where they *bring* it. That's not to say a character cannot be reactive, in part—each character is not a divine being with perfect and supreme will. A character acts, and the world (often through other characters) pushes back. And she is forced to contend with those oppositional reactions—but even in that, she is acting in return.

We've all met characters who don't feel instrumental, who feel like they could be replaced by a person made of balloons or a sexy hat rack. The plot keeps elbowing them this way and that, and it's totally inorganic. They don't feel like characters on a quest so much as they feel like characters dragged behind a pickup truck. When the plot pushes on active characters, they don't fall over. They don't let it happen. They respond and push back. Reactive should never mean passive.

- **PLOT EXISTS BECAUSE OF THE CHARACTER'S ACTIONS.** To say it again, characters do shit, and they say shit. And the story unfolds from this. They make decisions in the world and the plot—the sequence of events as revealed to the audience—unfolds from those decisions. Too many stories (particularly those of new writers) seem to give the "camera" (i.e., the perspective we take through the story) the agency—in other words, the plot is the point, and the characters are just woven in and out of it. This leaves us with a lot of pomp and circumstance, but little connection to the world—we know stuff is happening, but without seeing character agency in play, we have little reason to care. It's external, like stapling the skeleton to the outside of a jellied bag of skin and organs and hair and calling it "human." That's not a human, that's an artificial monster who can be given life only through judicious application of lightning. We like to think of a plot as external, but it's not. Like the skeleton, it is internal—and often invisible. It is controlled by the characters. It does not control them.

Look at the entire scope of history.

It's human. It's driven by humans. It's changed by humans. Sure, yes, you have things like volcanoes erupting and floods and other natural apocalypses that force humans to react—but even then, the *history* is the response. The *history* is in what the lava or the floodwaters buried and what can yet be revealed. History is a series of human choices and errors.

Just like your story.

Give the characters agency. Let them do things and say things. Give them power to shape the narrative. If you've ever felt like the characters are somehow "ruining the plot" or not acting in accordance to what you need them to do—that means you've been making plot the driver and the characters merely the passengers in the car. *Characters* are the ones who need to be driving—and, in many cases, it's a lot of characters all wrestling for the wheel of the car. Characters without agency feel like props. Characters *with* agency are characters who do the work for you, who create the story and, better yet, are damned interesting to watch.

STRONG FEMALE CHARACTERS

Beware the phrase 'strong female character.'

It's a great idea, in theory. We should, of course, be striving to make strong female characters, right? Like Trinity in the *Matrix*! Like Wyldstyle in *The LEGO Movie*! Like most of the ladies in *The Lord of the Rings* and *The Hobbit*. These ladies, boy howdy, they sure do kick some ass. KI-YAA. HI-YAA. Punch! Shoot! Pyoo pyoo! They're strong because they can punch a dude in the face.

Right? Wrong. *Strength* in this regard should refer to the depth and complexity of the character, not to whether or not she can kick a vampire's head off or fly a starfighter. The problem with a number of the women characters above are that they contain very little *agency*. Their stories are reflective of the male characters—they die to make the men sad; they swoon to make the men fall in love. They are levers to leverage the dudes into action. But they themselves are not pushing on the plot. They're fodder. They're sexy action figures. That's all.

Give the female characters—give *all* the characters—agency in the story. Let them all have problems, solutions, wants, and fears, and let them act on those things as independent architects within the narrative.

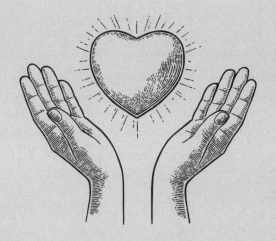

Interlude

THE THIRD RULE

The small story always matters more than the big story.

That's it. That's the rule.

We don't really care about the big story. We *think* we do. We think we want the ZOLWANG EMPIRE to fall to the GLORIOUS REPUBLIC OF FRONG, and we want the mighty HEROFACE JOHNSON[1] to get ahold of the SACRED SWORD OF DRAGON-MURDERING, and all this sounds fun and fine and important. We think we care about the Empire versus the Rebel Alliance, we think we care about Spider-Man versus the Vulture, we think we care about Buffy versus the Vampires.

But we don't. Not really. Not *deeply*.

What we care about is the small story embedded in there, the small story that's the beating heart of a larger one. We care about

---

[1] Coming soon, my new novel: HEROFACE JOHNSON AND THE FRONG OF ZOLWANG, BOOK FOUR IN THE DRAGON-MURDERER TRILOGY.

the characters and their personal drama. We care about their families, their loved ones, their struggles to feel normal, their attempts to do right in the face of wrong. We care about Buffy wanting to fall in love and hang out with her friends and not fail out of school. We care that the villains fighting Spider-Man are often connected to him personally, and that they reflect some aspect of his troubled journey from a geeky high school student to a city-saving mutant. We care about John McClane wanting to get his family back. We care about the friendships that form between Luke, Leia, and Han.

We care because *they* care.

We care because *their* story is *our* story. Our story is one of friendships and family, of love lost and jealousy made, of birth and death and everything in-between.

A big story without a smaller story has all the substance of a laser light show. It's pretty. It's dazzling. And it's very, very empty.[2]

Look for the little story.

Look for the story about people.

Then you can wrap it in a generous swaddling of space ninjas and swamp monsters and explodey-boom-boom-pyoo-pyoo-zap.

---

[2] As noted earlier in the book, one could argue that the failure of the Star Wars prequels is due in part because the trilogy takes too long to get to the *human* aspects—the small story!—and spends way too long dealing with trade disputes and Jedi prophecies and Midichlorian counts. By the time we start to care, it's already the third movie. Further, it's arguably why *Revenge of the Sith* works better despite the narrative problems carried in from the first two—it's more about fundamental human problems. It cleaves closer to the smaller story of Anakin, Padme, and their other relationships, and it remembers that all the galactic conflict prophecy stuff is really just hullabaloo (i.e., set dressing to contextualize the smaller story).

Damn Fine Story

Chapter Three

STRANGE ARRANGEMENTS: OR, HOW YOUR NARRATIVE GARDEN GROWS

Here's a story for you.

Recently, my family and I took a vacation to Maui. I know, I know—we live miserable lives. It was wretched—a veritable *purgatory* full of vicious warmth and vengeful rainbows. All that sand. All those palm trees.

Ew. Yuck. *Bleh*.

It was basically Hell.

Regardless of the breadth and depth of our tropical torture, one night we went to Hoʻokipa Beach on the North Shore to check out the *honu*[1] that gather there every afternoon and evening. They come struggling up the beach with all the velocity and eagerness of constipation, gathering amongst the rocks and looking like rocks themselves. And then a person shows up to rope off the TURTLE SLUMBERING AREA to make sure people don't go galloping up to the turtles for selfies.[2]

We went onto the beach, found about 40 turtles chilling out, took some photos, and so forth. Our son, B-Dub, played in the sand with a couple local boys, and we settled in for the sunset.

Down a bit from where we were, though, stood a dog.

This dog was a lean, long-snouted dog—a mutt of some kind, black fur, a bit of a hound look. The dog stood right at the edge of the ocean, on the rocks that separated the sand from the sea, staring out.

Now, Hoʻokipa Beach is known for a lot of things. It's known for the turtles, yes, but it's even *more* famous for the surfers and windsurfers. At any given time, there are a dozen or more out there on the waves.

The dog stood there, watching the surfers. Diligently. Nose pointed forward. Standing, never sitting. As if holding vigil.

Sometimes the tide, eager and aggressive, would crash up onto the rocks and pull the dog into the water. The dog, unfazed, would hop right back onto shore, take his place, and resume his watch.

The sun began to set. Evening bled bright across the horizon.

One of the first surfers came in from the water. The dog's tail began wagging with furious canine glee. As the surfer came up onto the beach, the dog ran over, happy, so happy—

---

[1] Green sea turtles

[2] I'm not sure exactly how you get the job of "Honu Minder," and I assume it does not pay well, but what a fabulous-sounding job. "What do you do for a living, Dan?" "I ROPE OFF THE TURTLES TO KEEP THEM SAFE FROM SELFIE-SEEKING GLORY-HOUND TOURISTS. YOU MESS WITH MY TURTLES, YOU SLEEP WITH THE FISHES."

And then he realized that this surfer was not his surfer.

So again he went back to his rock. Again he endured the waves.

Another surfer came up and, once more, the dog ran over only to discover that this was not his surfer. As the sky darkened, this cycle repeated again and again. A surfer would land. The dog would go. And, disappointed, the dog would plod sadly back to his tide-splashed perch.

The sun dipped in glorious fashion behind the West Maui Mountains, setting the sky on fire before bleeding wine across its surface to extinguish the flames. I have photo after photo of the dog standing there, waiting—

Waiting for what I began to believe was a surfer that would never come. Why, then, was the dog here? Why did the dog think every surfer was his friend, his master, his way home? How long would the dog stay here? Is the dog here every day? A narrative crept in at the margins: The dog came here with his surfer owner one day, and the surfer went out, the dog stood vigil—and the surfer never came home. The surfer drowned. Or ditched the dog. Either way, now the dog was left in his own kind of purgatory, the purgatory of an animal who believes that one day his friend will return.

I started to look around for someone to ask. A local, maybe. They would know the dog's true story. Already the sky was a deep purple. Evening was here, and night was soon to come. And the dog remained.

As I searched for someone, though, two more surfers came in. The last of the batch. Two women came up the beach, surfboards under one arm as they held hands. They stayed out late, the last of the last, coming in under the cover of almost darkness.

The dog turned his head toward them. His tail stiffened.

I thought, is this it? Are *they* his people?

The dog raced over toward what I feared was another batch of disappointment. He hurried over, and the two women greeted him as many of the surfers had—because who doesn't like a happy dog running up to them?—and then the dog turned away once more.

My heart sank.

The dog ran *not* to the rocks, however, but up the steps exiting the beach. He waited for the two women on the steps, tail wagging.

They were, in fact, his people. They got him in a truck. They drove away. Huzzah and hooray.

The end.

Cue applause, tears, joy, whatever it is you have in you.

Now, we're going to do the horrible thing where we take this story and we slop it up onto the metal slab, and we take our narrative scalpels and we slice it open. We *dissect* it.

And, in this case, we're looking at one particular component:

The arrangement of the bones.

When I tell you the story, I know the end of it. I know this dog that has waited and waited and waited *will* be paid for his vigilance. I know the dog has owners and isn't just waiting for the ghost of some dead surfer. I know the dog isn't alone, bereft of friend and master.

I didn't know it *at the time*. But I know it when I tell this story.

And in telling the story, I don't give that part away up front. Because to give that part away is to ruin the story. I'm a jerk. I'm trying to upset you. I'm *actively aiming* to stoke your emotions and take you on at least a smaller version of the emotional journey I went through worrying about this silly beach dog who kept getting pulled into the water, maybe waiting for a master who would never come. It's like making you watch a horror movie—I know where the scares are, and now I want to see if they scare *you* the same way they scared *me*.

Stories are like that. We take you on a journey, like I said in the last interlude, to make you *feel* and make you *think*. Nobody said I'm trying to make you feel good all the time. Nobody said I'm trying to make you think only happy thoughts. Stories drag you through the mud of multiple emotions and through the thorn-tangle of thinky thoughts.

The way I accomplish that in *this* story is, in part, through the arrangement. If I tell the story with the happy ending up front, it completely guts the stuffing right out of it. The story becomes spineless and unnecessary. You know the end, and the payoff is ruined.

The arrangement matters. It matters that I know the ending but tell the story as if I don't. It's *vital* that I play the magic trick as if I don't know where the rabbit is coming from—storytellers are, after all, practiced liars, and my job is to guide you through the journey, not fast-forward to the end. Part of the journey is about me asking questions and then withholding the answers for as long as you can stand it. It's like some kind of tantric narrative magic: Withhold the emotional orgasm for as great a time as possible.

Now, in some cases, telling you the end *is* how you generate the question—and the question is everything, as it's what pulls you through the tale.[3] In a certain story, if I tell you the ending first— that the protagonist died and maybe even who killed him—that creates new questions. Why did he die? What caused his death? Who killed him, or if we already know who, what was the motive for that murder? Again, the arrangement maximizes my ability as a storyteller to make you think and feel. If I had told you up front that the dog finds his owner, I would have undercut the only question I could really bring you in that short tale; if I tell you about a murder, it generates new questions. The arrangement of the story should be there to generate questions rather than offer quick answers.

The arrangement of your story—how you tell it and in what order you present the sequence of events—is key to all of this. It matters so much, it can ruin the best story and elevate the worst.

Let's see how.

------

[3] The question mark is shaped like a hook, after all …

SPOILER WARNINGS

Please hold still while I get up on my soapbox.

struggles to climb up on a soapbox

Man, soapboxes are slippery. Probably all that soap. Whatever. I'll stay down here and just yell really loud.

DO NOT SPOIL STORIES FOR PEOPLE. Don't ever do it. Be nice. Be thoughtful. Don't tell them what happened on that show, or in this movie, or in the pages of that comic book or novel. It's disrespectful to them.

And it's disrespectful to the storyteller. Because here's the deal: That whole *arrangement* thing I'm talking about in this chapter? It's intentional. We write the stories we write in such a way so as to provoke mystery and conflict and *reaction*. We want people to walk the maze. But when you spoil something, you short-circuit that. You knock down walls and let them walk straight through to the big moments—moments we work hard to orchestrate. You cut through tension we worked to escalate. You ruin it. It's like telling how a magic trick works before anybody has the chance to see it. It's like pooping in the soup. Don't poop in the soup. Stop that. Be nice.

Respect the story.

UNITS OF NARRATIVE MEASUREMENT

If we want to talk about arrangement, we have to talk about the pieces being arranged. We need to get on the same page and understand exactly what the building blocks of narrative are.

The units of narrative measurement are these, from smallest to largest:

- **BEAT.** A beat is a moment within the story that comprises, roughly, an action or a dialogue or some other consequential moment. Example: The moment Leia gives R2D2 the Death Star plans at the fore of *A New Hope* is a beat. So, too, is when John McClane drops a dead body out of a window onto Al Powell's cop car.

- **SCENE.** A scene is a collection of beats held together by a relatively consistent setting (meaning, it doesn't tend to *leave* the setting). A scene tends to have a common purpose in that it advances the story in one direction and does not cut away from that setting, cast, or purpose. In *The Empire Strikes Back*, one scene is when both Luke and his Tauntaun are mauled by a gropey Wampa and dropped into the snow. In *The Princess Bride*, the entire swordfight between Inigo and the Man in Black comprises a scene (with each "move" in the fight—physical and rhetorical!—being a beat).

- **SEQUENCE.** A sequence is an agglomeration of scenes that smush together to form a larger common purpose. You can be more flexible with setting and location here—the different scenes in a sequence will jump location and include different characters. In *The Empire Strikes Back*, several scenes go toward the act of finding and rescuing Luke from the Wampa—the rebels learning Luke didn't come back, Han going out into the snow, the docking doors closing (and Chewie's oh-so-mournful Wookiee wail), Luke saving himself from the Wampa, Han sticking him inside a steaming sack of Tauntaun innards, and Rogue Two finding them the next morning. These are all individual scenes that go toward the "Luke Rescue" sequence. What follows is the "Empire Attacks Hoth" sequence—snowspeeders and stompy AT-ATs[4] and escaping transports. Each sequence is built of scenes, fills a larger narrative purpose, and has its own rise and fall of tension.

- **ACT.** An act is a larger chunk of narrative meat that represents the story moving in one direction until it pivots in a new direction. In other words, each act establishes its own status quo and

---

[4] I pronounce this at-at, not ay-tee, ay-tee, and the people who pronounce it the latter way are monsters wearing human faces. WE ARE ONTO YOU, MONSTERS, YOUR COSTUME HAS BEEN EXPOSED AND YOUR MALEVOLENT RUSE IS AT AN END.

when that status quo is shattered, a new act begins. Sometimes acts are separated by a huge shift in location, or time, or even in the cast or characters or theme that binds it all together.

In *Die Hard*, the first act takes John (and us, by proxy) through the discomfort of flying, landing, getting a limo, going to the party, meeting all the new people, finding his wife, and on and on—it establishes the new status quo for him, which is being a New York cop trapped in a building full of California executives. And then the film shatters that status quo when Gruber and the Gang show up, and McClane is called to action in his bare feet. That marks the beginning of the second act. And that second act goes until another shift in the status quo—John has alerted the police, he's stolen the detonators, and Gruber's mission is now not only to break the locks on the safe but to hunt down McClane and those detonators. Every act is a pivot, a major transitional point where the stakes are either seriously raised or transformed into something else. An act breaks when the status quo shifts in a big way—big enough to reshape the narrative, the stakes, the threat.

So, to recap:

- Beats build scenes.
- Scenes build sequences.
- Sequences build acts.
- And acts build a story.

Now, some of these terms come out of theater and film. There, the building blocks have concrete benefits—you *need* definite signals to know when locations should change, when you need to block different action on the stage, when different characters enter or exeunt, and so on and so forth. In theater, especially, these changes aren't always clear to the audience—stage sets have their limits—so the notes of "Scene" and "Act" in the programs help them follow along. Further, modern film is given over to a theoretical (not always practiced) pattern of the dreaded (gasp) three-act-structure. You get eight sequences packed into three acts, with a series of predefined beats and scenes along the way.

And TV, well, it has its own act structure, which might be limited depending on the network where it will air—for example, a lot of television is given over to commercial breaks, and further, a lot of television is *paid* for by those commercial breaks. As such, television is sometimes written around those breaks—an episode is structured in just such a way to keep you there through the break. An individual act is the space between one commercial break and the next, which is why each act tends to end on a so-called "act-out," where you get some moment of tension or mystery or shocking revelation—OH MY GOD STEVE IS DEAD, WHOA THE CAR JUST CRASHED, WOW SHE'S ABOUT TO LEARN A SECRET ABOUT MARY— so you are hungry enough to come back to the story once the commercial break is ended.[5]

The number of commercial breaks, therefore, determines how many acts fit into the episode, and different networks have different numbers of commercial breaks.

Some television shows don't have commercial breaks at all, and so the act breaks are given over to greater flexibility, which is why, maybe, a network like HBO or Netflix creates what is perceived as a higher, more artful form of storytelling. (This isn't universally true, of course.)

Comics, too, operate a bit like television. The structure is episodic but doesn't have to contend with the invasiveness of advertising. (Yes, a comic *has* advertisements present, but getting past them requires no more investment than flipping the page.) There, each comic essentially serves as a single act, getting us from the start of

---

[5] A good example of this is in reality TV. When you watch a reality show, you will note that just as you're about to get to a moment of revelation—*who won this round of* Food Battle? *Which home will they choose on* Houseboat Hunters? *Which person will they vote to be covered in biting otters?*—the cameras immediately cut to a commercial, leaving you hungry for more.

the issue to the end, and ideally bridging out in a way that makes us eager to buy the next issue—putting it on our pull list at the local comic book shop. Comics too sometimes follow a "W" format, in which we alternate between *action scenes* and *non-action scenes* (which could include character development, dialogue, clue-finding, plot revelations, etc.) to keep the story moving at a brisk pace. (The "W" shape is just meant to show the jagged up-and-down of action/non-action—each peak is action, each valley subtracts the action.)

What about theater? Well, Shakespeare's plays were five acts long. Some plays are three (first act: exposition; second act: complication; third act: resolution). Others are seven. Others still are just one act (aka, the one-act play, a loose equivalent of a short story in dramatic form).

And *films* are given over to a theoretical (not always practiced) pattern of the dreaded (gasp) three act-structure. You get eight sequences packed into three acts, with a series of predefined beats and scenes along the way. In practice, they generally have four acts, not three, with the longer second act broken in half by the midpoint of the story.

The acts in a three-act film structure work out to 25 percent/50 percent/25 percent of the story, respectively (or, in a two-hour movie, thirty minutes for the first act, sixty for the second, thirty for the last). As in theater, film roughly follows a path of exposition for the first act, complication for the second act, and climax for the final act.

In novels … well, novels don't *technically* have acts at all, in the sense that novels are given over to no rigorous format. That said, certainly we've seen books whose chapters are arranged into larger sections, and one could argue that these constitute acts. And one could further argue that each chapter equates to a scene or a sequence. As with most arrangements, the acts pair together, pivoting into each other until culminating in the final act. Sometimes three, sometimes five, sometimes seven. Really, it demands as many acts as you choose for it to have. A book with a more mythic narrative might have architecture that looked like this:

Intro → Problem/Attack → Initial Struggle → Complications → Failed Attempts → Major Crisis → Climax and Resolution.

Some novelists or screenwriters cleave to the monomyth, which takes us through Joseph Campbell's seventeen steps of a hero's journey—and very roughly adds up to this structure, divided into three acts:

ACT ONE: DEPARTURE

The Call to Adventure → Refusal of the Call → Supernatural Aid → The First Threshold → Belly of the Whale.

ACT TWO: INITIATION

The Road of Trials → Meeting with the Goddess → Temptation → Atonement with the Father → Apotheosis → The Ultimate Boon.

ACT THREE: RETURN

Refusal of the Return → The Magic Flute → Rescue from Without → The Crossing of the Return Threshold → Master of Two Worlds → Freedom to Live.

You can see this shape in pop culture storytelling all the time. George Lucas used it in Star Wars (*A New Hope* is literally about Luke's departure from the world he knew, *The Empire Strikes Back* is about his initiation into the Jedi arts, and the third story is *literally* called *Return of the Jedi*.) Harry Potter is another version of a character who is called to adventure but refuses it (or rather, has it refused for him by his horrible adopted family, the Dursleys), only to be drawn to the adventure anyway, entering a world of magic and mystery where he must navigate issues surrounding his parents to defeat an ultimate evil.

Beyond Campbell, there's also Vladimir Propp's thirty-one-step morphology of the folktale, which I'm not going to extrapolate here because we all have better things to do.[6]

Size breeds complexity, too, so the larger your story—even if it's just a series of smaller stories or episodes—the more you have to consider how exactly the arrangement will best serve the tale and the audience. And yet, paradoxically, as complicated as the arrangement may become, at the end of the day it's still easy enough to break down into three parts:

First: Intro, Problem/Attack
Second: Initial Struggle, Complications, Failed Attempts
Third: Major Crisis, Climax, and Resolution

Or, even simpler, it breaks down to:

Beginning.

Middle.

And **End.**

It's all very simple.[7]

What, exactly, is the point of telling you all this? Will it help provide you with a blueprint by which to design your stories? Maybe. It can. You wouldn't be the first writer to use the Monomyth to tell a story, and certainly not the last. The point, though, is less about these very specific patterns and more about how there are a great *many* very specific patterns and none of them needs to be very specific to *you*. You can use them or discard them at your leisure. You can borrow from one and from another and find your own way through. You can also ask yourself: How exactly could the story shape of a comic book influence the story shape of a novel, or vice versa? The goal is to simply have you *consider* these things: both that story is flexible and also that familiar patterns emerge through these divergent shapes.

---

[6] Google is your friend!
[7] And all very confusing.

THE COURSES OF DINNER

Meals tell stories, too. Not overtly, of course—it's more that you're trying to escalate and complicate the flavors and, often enough, bring some kind of narrative to the meal. ("This meal will explore the spiritual significance of the halibut and the ennui that plagues all the fish under the sea.")

An eleven-course dinner might look like this:

Amuse-bouche → aperitif → appetizer → palate cleanser → main course → cheese → palate cleanser → dessert → coffee → digestif → coma.

The point here is not to give you a model to use to specifically shape the story, but to understand the rhythm of shaping a story, and to see how a story rises and falls, to see how it builds to one taste and then changes directions.

ANATOMY OF A SCENE

Bricks can build houses just as beats can build stories, but at the end of the day, it's not the individual bricks that matter. It's how they add up. And the bricks of a story add up to two vital architectural components of a house: They make walls, and (via the walls) they make rooms.

Every room is different and has different functions, but each is subject to a few fundamental truths that make them effective: They need doorways in and out for access. They need enough space to perform function. They need vents for heating and cooling. They need a stable floor, a trustworthy ceiling, and so on and so forth.

Scenes are also like this. Each scene is different. They have different functions. But they also have some traits in common that generally make them more effective, and these traits should be kept in mind:

1. **A SCENE ALWAYS HAS CHARACTERS.** Or, at least one character. A scene without characters is a photograph of scenery. (Note: There is an argument that I'll make later that suggests a good way to handle your setting and your storyworld is to treat *them* very much like characters too, to earn you as much juice from the squeeze as possible.)

2. **A SCENE ALWAYS HAS PURPOSE.** When telling a story, there exists the stuff going on right there upon the page, and then there exists the stuff way above it, in the clouds, in *your* storytelling head. *You* need to know why this scene exists. You have to know what the scene does and how it earns its place. Defend it. Identify not why it must happen but rather *why the audience needs to see it*. (Remember: A story is as much about what the audience doesn't see as what it does. We can define plot as the sequence of events *as revealed to the audience*, so what you include needs to be purpose driven.) Is it telling us something about the characters? Is it moving events forward with a necessary tentpole moment? Is it delivering a key piece of information to the audience—and to the characters, as well? A scene needn't merely have one purpose, either. It can pull double duty. It can say something about theme as well as move the plot forward. It can give us a crucial character moment while also reinforcing mood.

3. **THE CHARACTERS IN A SCENE ALSO HAVE PURPOSE.** They're not simply set dressing. They don't just stick their thumbs up their no-no holes and stare blankly into the camera. Make it a point to identify what every character in a scene is doing and what their priorities are: What are their goals? Do they serve a role true to themselves, and do they also have a role in the action on the page or on the screen? One way to help you identify their goals is to get to the next item on the list. …

4. **THE SCENE ALWAYS HAS A PROBLEM.** And I don't mean a problem like a *flaw*—it's not the Death Star, you don't need to design a wall outlet that some precocious young Jedi janitor can blow

up with a Force-powered Swiffer mop. I mean that just as every character has a problem to solve, so too is a scene given over to some kind of problem, conflict, question, or drama. A scene without conflict is a scene without tension … which is to say, a scene that gives us no reason to read it. What are the obstacles? What is the driving push and pull that gives us cause to keep on through the scene? Note: The problem may or may not be related to the characters' own, character-based problems. Further, the scene may or may not solve the problem intrinsic to it—the problem may persist or may even become worse.

5. **A SCENE HAS A BEGINNING, A MIDDLE, AND AN END.** It has an arc of its own. It has shape. And in this way, you'll start to see that a scene is a microcosm. Just as you might note how an individual atom is not all that structurally different from our entire galaxy, you might also note how the structure of a scene needs to somewhat mirror the shape of a story. More to the point, a scene is not just a vignette. It isn't a snapshot in time or a meandering moment. It starts, it gains momentum and complexity, it has stakes and problems, and then it ends, carrying us to the next scene.

6. **THE SCENE SHOULD BEGIN AS LATE AS POSSIBLE.** Meaning, it doesn't begin until something happens. It begins when it *needs* to. That's vague, I know, but ask yourself when writing a scene: Can this start deeper in the thick of things? Can you trim some of the fat from the front of it? Some scenes gain tension by playing out—seeing characters build up and into the scene, slowly, surely. There exists strategic value in giving a scene some oxygen—some room to breathe. (More on that a little later in this chapter.) But it's also vital not to waste the audience's time. If a scene jumps in too early—imagine if *A New Hope* started ten minutes earlier, before the Empire attacked—it not only wastes the audience's time, it also takes up space in a novel or a script that could have gone to more impactful, eventful storytelling. You want to maximize the narrative potential of the piece, and

that means being judicious about giving a scene just enough room: Too much room and the audience will find themselves wandering, lost and bewildered, uncertain of the purpose.

7. **A SCENE SHOULD END IN A WAY THAT ENTICES US TO KEEP GO-ING.** That means it ends on an unresolved conflict, or it brings up a new problem, or it introduces a new question. Maybe it puts a character in danger. Maybe it suggests a coming change, foreshadowing a new threat. One way or another, it's your job to end the scene with a doorway that invites the audience to continue on. You are baiting the readers to keep on through the tale. (All this assumes, of course, that we're not talking about the final scene of the story, though even there we want to leave the audience wanting a little more—satisfied, yes, but eager to return.)

8. **A SCENE ONLY WORKS IF THE AUDIENCE HAS THE NECESSARY INFORMATION TO CONTINUE.** Every scene is a new opportunity to lose the audience, and one of the best (worst) ways to lose the audience is to confuse them. Which means the audience either needs the information that will allow them to contextualize and parse what's happening in a scene, or you need to provide it throughout the scene as it unfolds. (Obviously the latter is necessary for the earliest scenes in a story because the audience doesn't come to the narrative fully informed—it's your job to introduce characters and situations as they come.) The longer the scene goes without the audience knowing what the hell is going on, the likelier it is that they'll fugue out and go raid the fridge or start dicking around on their iPhone.

Now, the key here is *necessary* information—not extraneous, redundant information. Every scene is metaphorically a dark room through which you're guiding your readers: You don't need to turn all the lights on, but you *do* need to hand them a flashlight. Although maybe it's a flashlight with a wobbly, flickering beam. Remember: A little information can go a long way.

Let's look at that opening scene of *A New Hope.* I probably don't even have to describe it to you, but just in case: A little Corellian ship launches through the void, followed by the massive, bladelike Imperial star destroyer in close pursuit. The Corellian ship is in trouble—laser fire,[8] alarms going off. We quickly zip onboard that ship to watch a couple of droids bumbling about, the golden one going on about how there will be "no escape for the princess this time," while soldiers gather, readying for combat.

This scene dumps us right in the thick of it. We don't get a lot of lead-up, and we are launched immediately into a nest of questions. Who is pursuing them? Who is being pursued and why? Who the hell is the princess, and wait, are those robots? We get a *little* bit of room to breathe with Threepio and Artoo conversing, and then a hard burst of taut-wire tension as the soldiers prepare for the ship to be boarded—

And when it is, it's laser fire and men down and the bleak, black imposing figure of the Imperial enforcer, Darth Vader.

When we look at it in terms of the scene elements above, we see: It has its characters.

Those characters have purpose in and out of the story: In story, the droids are there to serve the needs of the princess, and out of story they are there as the audience's eyes and ears; Vader's role in story is to hunt the Death Star plans, and beyond it, to give us a face for this frightening, autocratic Empire; Leia's role in the story is to resist the Empire and to hide the Death Star plans, and out of the story she is both heroine and victim, the face of the Rebel Alliance.

The *scene* has purpose, too, in that it establishes mystery through incomplete information (that single phrase, "no escape for the princess this time," establishes for us a mysterious figure of royalty who must be onboard, and who *clearly* has a history of these sort of scrapes—it's one line of dialogue with a whole lot packed into it) and gets us excited for what's to come. Plus, the scene has *conflict*

---

[8] pyoo-pyoo-pyoo!

in that the ship is being boarded by a clearly sinister and oppressive enemy who has to be resisted.

It has a beginning (they're being boarded!), a middle (droids conversing and bumbling, soldiers preparing for boarding), and an ending (explosion! lasers! Vader! droid escape!). It doesn't begin before it needs to and, further, when it ends, it does so in a way that leaves us wanting more. We have questions. We want to know what comes next. Vader's here, we haven't even met this princess character yet, and whoa hey wait, where are those droids going?

In the next scene, we receive our answer: The mystery deepens as Leia (our erstwhile princess) gives the droids something and boots them off the ship. Then *another* scene, with Vader encountering Leia, and all of that adds up to the film's first sequence of scenes, which comprises the boarding and capture of Princess Leia's ship while the droids escape with what we learn are the plans to something called a "Death Star."[9]

Of course, different scenes are differently executed—but still tick our boxes. Go to the scene in *The Princess Bride* where Inigo and the Man in Black square off with swordplay.

Obviously, it has its characters: Inigo and the Man in Black.

The characters each have their purpose, and that purpose is clearly spelled out for us: The Man in Black is in pursuit of the kidnappers, and Inigo is there to prevent his pursuit. And so, they do what they must, which is cross blades. But also, they talk, and that's very important because … the *conversation* gives the scene its purpose, too. It introduces both of these characters. Yes, we've met them both before, but up until this point Inigo was mostly a quippy background player, and we didn't yet realize that the Man in Black is the Dread Pirate Roberts who is *also* Westley the Farm Boy. Further, not only do we have introductions, but we have a lead-in to Inigo's own

---

[9] Pro-tip for the Empire: You guys might want to learn the value of euphemistic language. I think the "Values Reinforcement Sphere" would've gone over a lot better than the "Death Star." Also, your Emperor looks like a wizened goblin-man, which can't be good for your image. The Empire needs a *serious* makeover.

problem, where he regales the Man in Black—and *us*, by proxy—with his tale of his father's demise at the hand of the six-fingered man.

Oh, the scene also gives us an awesome sword fight.[10]

Point is, it's a lot of fun, we see the mastery of each character, we receive intros to their story, etc., etc.

It has a beginning (Inigo helps Westley to the top of the cliff they've both climbed in their pursuit), a middle (they talk, then begin to fight, and Inigo confesses he has been using his left hand but is not left-handed), and an end (a reversal of fortune as the Man in Black *also* confirms he has been using his left hand but is not left-handed, thus besting the Spaniard and knocking him unconscious).

Now, the scene takes a little while to build—it allows some oxygen right at the front, loading it with exposition. In a less-masterful hand, that might feel clunky, but writer William Goldman and the performers keep it peppy, witty, engaging. Even during that time of oxygen, we are granted the tension to know what's coming: The conversation is simply stalling the inevitable fight. That's important. The oxygen works because we know the stakes—we know what each wants, and we know what must occur for each to get it. We see the metaphorical sword dangling above the whole scene, we just don't know when it'll fall—or on whom. So the scene begins just where it needs to, and its slower build is purposeful and elegant.

When it ends, it ends with the Man in Black still in pursuit—onward he goes, and we do not know the future of the unconscious Spaniard *or* how the Man in Black will fare against the giant he is soon to face. Those are two big question marks that keep us running through the tale.

TRANSITIONS

One piece of storytelling that doesn't get its due (at least from where I'm sitting) is the subject of transitions.

---

[10] Maybe *all* scenes of dialogue should contain awesome sword fights.

By transitions, I mean the bridges between story elements that take us from one place to the next. Maybe this bridges a gap in time, or is a line drawn from one setting to another, or is simply just about moving the overall story forward, scene by scene.

They're a source of great frustration even for me because they're ultimately vital and yet, at the same time, feel so damned *unnecessary*. It's like, take a look at the human body. The cool parts are obvious: a head, some arms, some legs, a sassy pair of buttocks.[11] But then you have all the *connecty* bits—like, have you ever taken a close look at your knee? Or worse, your elbow? *God*, the elbow is just some ugly, anatomical aberration—it's flappy skin and a gingerroot knob underneath, and then buried inside there you have the funny bone, which is easily the worst named part of the body because hitting it even lightly feels like *you've been hit in the arm by a hammer*. It's like brain freeze, except for your entire arm. It's dumb. The whole elbow is dumb and makes me sad.

And that's often how I feel about writing transitions.

They're the elbows of fiction.

And yet—*and yet!*—the elbow is a fundamental part of the arm. Without it, you'd just have a stiff broomstick with a hand at the end of it. You'd be a cheap action figure who could never bring a cup of coffee or donut to your lips, who could never hug another human, or punch another human, or really do anything except point like you're starring in a new version of *Invasion of the Body Snatchers*.

Transitions, also, are often like that: knobby and inelegant, but necessary.

So let's establish some ground rules for making your transitions as elegant as possible.

First, okay, no, not *every* transition scene is necessary. Sometimes you can just jump from this part to the next—you don't need the literal bridge where people are driving or walking or otherwise

---

[11] Well, at least *mine* are sassy, I can't speak for you.

conveying themselves (and the story) from scene to scene or from sequence to sequence. As with all things, if the transition feels non-essential, cut it. (The best way to determine this, in my experience, is to write it and let it sit—and cut it during revisions. If the story still reads well without the transition, so be it.)

Second, if you *do* need one, keep it mercifully short. In a novel, this can be literally a paragraph at the end or fore of a chapter. In a script, it can be just a line or two of description. Just as a movie might begin with an establishing shot that shouts HERE LOOK, IT'S NEW YORK CITY, a transitional component can be characters doing something simple to get us from one place to the next. It needn't be fancy; brutal efficiency is the name of the game.

Third, if the transition needs to be longer, make the damn thing sing for its supper—bump it up from transition to proper scene. What I mean is *force it to be useful*. Double-duty time! The transitional scene can somehow further the story by deepening a character's arc, giving us insight into the character, driving home the story's theme, or revealing a crucial piece of information. Make it into a scene that also happens to take your characters from one place to the next.

Want a good example of a transition in film? *Casablanca*. It's an oldie, but, goddamn, is it a goodie! In that movie, the introduction of the Nazis transitions to the introduction of Rick by drawing us inside from the street and winding through the crowded establishment of Rick's cafe. It gives us a sense of the storyworld and the central setting of the film, and it does so swiftly and with great, elegant care. Further, it's enticing and welcoming as it draws us in. It makes us feel like a *part* of the story.

If you want a pretty good example of stories that largely eschew transitional scenes? Star Wars comes to mind. All of the films keep it speedy and pulpy, moving us from THIS PLACE to OH WE'RE HERE NOW to OH, SHIT, LASERS[12] without much more than

---

[12] pyoo-pyoo-pyoo!

screen wipes as merciless as a hand brushing dirt off a shoulder.[13] Point is, Star Wars movies don't spend a lot of time getting the characters from here to there—they mostly just put them there and expect us, the audience, to keep up. It can be a little jarring, but it also has the advantage of keeping us on our feet and at attention. It also became a hallmark of the series' style.

CREATING TENSION: THE RHYTHM OF FIRE AND OXYGEN

Let's dial it back a little bit and consider the single and smallest item of storytelling measurement: *the beat*. At the basic, most fundamental level, think of each moment in your story as a heartbeat. When you're calm, your pulse is a slow, steady beat. When excited, it throbs and jitters. When you're terrified, it goes into tachycardia and everything feels like electricity and you might pee your britches.

I mean, ha ha, I've never peed *my* britches when I'm scared, no matter what the pictures on the Internet say.

clears throat

Storytelling is often a push between order and chaos—a battle between oxygen and the fire that consumes it. Stories breathe. And story*tellers* pump oxygen—air, precious air—into the story because the audience needs to be able to breathe with the story. As audience members, we need moments to look around, to understand characters, to take the measure of where we are, who we're with, and why. And then, as storytellers, we burn up all that precious oxygen with sweet, cleansing flame. Heat and light! Melting fixtures and choking smoke! Excitement and horror! Fire! *Wonderful fire.*

Sorry, got a little carried away there—the glint of chaotic firelight dancing in my eyes again, is it? Let's get back to the oxygen—the sense of order in a story. Look at it this way: When you have oxygen,

---

[13] Or an elbow. Stupid elbows.

you have room to breathe slowly and completely. You have time. You get comfortable and calm. You can stretch your legs.

Stories need that. We need the moment of John McClane balling up his toes on a carpet. We need the moment where he's sitting there, talking with Al Powell over the radio during what will surely be a short respite from all the machine-gunning and exploding. We need Buffy to talk about school and boys with Willow. We need Luke to hunker down with Obi-Wan or Yoda and learn about life, his father, and the Force.

Stories need oxygen.

But when *all* you have is oxygen, the story can grow indolent—it gets sleepy, sluggish, overly thoughtful. It becomes *too* safe.

It gets *boring*.

And to hell with boring.

So, to all that buildup of oxygen, you add heat and fuel, and you get the fun part: *fire*. Fire is exciting. It's conflict, it's drama, it's agitation. And, obviously, I don't mean literal fire, I mean the metaphorical fire of what happens when you take the safety and the status quo of the characters and you put that in jeopardy. You burn up their safe space. You close off their exits. You force them into a fight-or-flight situation: either stay and contend with the flames or escape to fresh air. John McClane is attacked anew. Darth Vader shows up on Cloud City. Buffy discovers her boyfriend has—oops!—turned evil for the thirty-seventh time. The fire is my favorite part. It's the part where you burn it all down, where you stoke the fuel and move the story. Characters—and, by proxy, the audience—can't get too comfortable for too long, so you need to add some heat.

Ah, but it can't *all* be fire, can it? When fire becomes the status quo, that's just a new kind of boring. Characters cannot live amongst the flames. More to the point, a story cannot be constant tension or conflict. When that happens, we grow numb to it. It fails to bring the same kind of heat and light that it once did. Life is about contrasts: Images exist because of the contrast between colors and between dark and light. We know the value of day because we lived through the night. Happiness elevates us because we know its opposite: grief. And conflict and tension only work if we have seen the characters experience safety.

The grim reality of storytelling is this: The audience wants the characters to be safe and happy, and our job as storytellers is to tease them with that safety and happiness ... and then ruin it. We are out to hurt them. Not constantly, oh, no, no, no. We always hand over the carrot and let them have a few bites before we finally deliver the stick. So we fill the space with the oxygen. ...

And then we start the fire.

This creates a pattern for us, right? Air and flame, air and flame. The oxygen is fuel for the fire, the fire consumes it, and so we need air once more. (Think back again to that "W" shape mentioned in regards to comics writing on page 90.) We stagger how much oxygen we need and how many fires we set, depending on the needs of the story—and it's this pattern that creates for us the rhythm.

So, back we go to the heartbeat: The narrative pulse is sometimes slow and steady, other times quickening until it feels like the story's heart is going to high kick its way through the breastbone and out of the chest. You can see this in some stories: *A New Hope* starts out right in the frying pan with the fire of Vader invading Leia's ship. Once the droids break out via escape pod to Tatooine ...

We are afforded some oxygen—some downtime in which to breathe as Goldenrod[14] and Artoo wander the sands and eventually separate, coming together once more to meet Luke and his family.

Ah, but then: conflict once more! Flames and oxygen in bursts: Tusken Raider attack, then breathe. A fight in the cantina, then breathe. Escape Tatooine in the Millennium Falcon ... and then, ahhh, breathe.

---

[14] Aka C-3PO, aka Threepio

As the film goes on, these beats come a bit faster, until the third act reveals the attack on the Death Star—there, the fire comes hot and heavy and only leaves enough oxygen for us to gulp in short bursts. Stories are like this: a constant ratchet-and-release of tension, the tightening of a spring, which then fires and relaxes once more.

This is pacing. This is rhythm. It's the tension and recoil of conflict into resolution and back into conflict once more. Pressure builds, steam releases. Then again, and again, and again, with variation as to how long the pressure builds and holds before release— and variation as to how long a period of release we as the audience are allowed to have. Think of the game Jenga: You remove one piece and, *if the tower remains standing*, everybody breathes a sigh of relief. Tension, release, tension, release, and with every block out, the tower gets wobblier and wobblier. Certainty fades as the whole thing teeters. We get less oxygen each time. The fire will burn hotter when next it fuels up. And because we know that, we begin to use our oxygen—our downtime—to anticipate the fire that's coming. Which means the air you give your story can be as much a tool to build tension as the fire—the fire is the release of tension. The oxygen is when we build the tension because, in our minds, we imagine what is to come. The oxygen also gives us more time to *care* about what's there: the characters, the mysteries, the details.

And it is our imagination that cultivates the greatest suspense. In that downtime grows impatience, fear, and excitement for what's to come. It might be conflict, drama, more questions, more answers, or maybe bears—we don't know, *maybe bears will come and eat us.*[15]

We use the arrangement of elements to achieve this. You can play with them to see what effect they earn. Longer beats at the start of slower scenes might start to coalesce into faster beats, tighter scenes, more exciting sequences. That's the most traditional arrangement, classic to most action or adventure movies. Though that's not to say

---

[15] Frankly, we probably deserve it.

it's all plodding and dull up front—*Die Hard* starts with a slower pace (in heartbeat terms, a calmer pulse) and goes up from there, but *A New Hope* begins in the thick of things, with the attack on the rebel ship: We start right off with a pretty fast pulse, and then it only accelerates, as here come lasers and stormtroopers and a brutal Sith lord with his Dark Side voodoo.

Great thing is, there exists no one pattern, no one arrangement, that earns you the best outcome. You gotta play with it. You have to experiment. It's like songs—some get right into it, others build up the tempo slow and easy, others stay slow the whole time and use that to languidly smother you underneath grief and sorrow. A kick-ass rock anthem might bring it down right in the middle, pulling back on the tempo—same way a roller coaster climbs its hill slowly and with dreadful, steady ease, building surely to the fast downward acceleration you know is coming.

This works at the microcosmic level and at larger levels. You play with fire and oxygen. You establish a rhythm by staggering beats, but you also do this by staggering scenes and sequences. Generally the simplest direction is one of escalation—although that also depends on how we define escalation.

Escalation means the intensification of events: Things get more intense, more violent, more heated, more whatever. A classic real-life version of escalation is the battle between two neighbors.

At our first house, a row home where we were, *erm*, uncomfortably close to our neighbors, we went outside one morning to discover *a series of inexplicable things.*

- **THING 1:** several pink paint stains on our front door, as if applied by paintball
- **THING 2:** a poster-board sign staked into our neighbor's lawn—a sign written in hasty scrawls of permanent marker depicting an ill-scribbled person *with a handgun* shooting little hyphenated

pee-pee bullets, and above that person, a message: BEWARE NUM ONE GOD

- **THING 3:** a cinder block in the middle of the road outside our house

My wife and I were left staggered by this bizarre trio of elements and objects that didn't quite ... connect. Paintball stains? Creepy sign? Cinder block?

This, then, was a moment of *oxygen* in the story as we stood there contemplating what had happened. Were we attacked? Did someone shoot our door, leave a scary sign on our neighbor's lawn, then put a cinder block in the road?

Fearful, we knocked on our neighbor's door—our neighbor was a woman, a decade or so older than us. She came out, and instantly I knew something was off, because when her gaze flicked over the *series of inexplicable things*, at no point did she seem concerned. We said, "Look, look," and we swept our arms out as if to behold this *series of inexplicable things*, and she laughed.

Our neighbor said, "I put those there."

"The cinder block?" we asked

She nodded. "People drive too fast on this road."

"The *sign*?" we asked.

She nodded. "I was warning people to stay off my property."

"The paintball splats?"

"Oh that wasn't me," she said. Turns out, our neighbor had gotten into an entirely *different* escalating battle with some kids who had at some point thrown a plastic soda bottle onto her lawn, and she chased after their car with a rake. They returned with paintball guns, accidentally hitting *our* house instead of hers. Her gun-carrying God[16] sign—and to a lesser degree, her cinder block—were messages to these vengeful litterers.

---

[16] NUM ONE GOD apparently meant NUMBER ONE GOD, I guess indicating there are other, less significant deities she chose not to call upon in her invocation of rage.

Up until that point, we had no reason to believe she was in any way a concern to us—she always seemed nice and, frankly, fairly together. She lived alone, sometimes with a teenage granddaughter (who was also very nice). But now, a new picture was forming: a picture of someone who, to convince people to slow down, would put a cinder block in the road. Someone who, to dissuade litterers, would threaten both GOD and GUNFIRE. Someone who invited paint-ballers to paint ball her damn house.

This was just the beginning.

One day, we caught people trespassing on our property, looking at our lawn furniture in our backyard in case we wanted to "sell it." Turns out, they were friends of hers who felt comfortable enough to wander onto our yard and size up our stuff for potential sale.

We responded by putting up a fence.[17]

She responded by putting up a fence all her own, sandwiched tight against our fence, which cost her money and time and did nothing except shrink her yard by a couple extra inches.

She had plumbing work done, and the plumbers would show up at 9 p.m. and work till the middle of the night, banging and hammering. We asked her to stop, and she just got louder, even after the plumbing work had been completed: playing music, stomping around, banging into things. Worse, one night she decided to burn a *giant bonfire* in her backyard—and, to be clear, our yards were about ten-people wide. We're not talking palatial estates, here. The fire was less than five feet from our very wooden, very flammable fence.

We called the fire department, which came and put her bonfire out. They cited her, because as it turns out, it's a really bad idea *and against code* to hold a conflagration pyre when your backyard is roughly the size of a postage stamp.

Next day, we caught her spraying our flower beds with weed killer.

Thankfully, at that point, by calling the police, we were able to cut that situation off at the knees. But we could've kept responding. And

---

[17] Good fences make good neighbors, according to Robert Frost.

responding would've meant escalating, and escalating would've meant ... I don't know, honestly. Broken windows? Rabid squirrels loosed into the other's kitchen? It's not hard to see how that gets worse and worse until it's two neighbors locked in *orbital bombardment*.

Another real-world example of escalation isn't the war between neighbors, but rather the war between nations. War begins with a border dispute, escalates to an assassination, and next thing you know political alliances are being tested, old enemies rise from the shadows, and *oh shit*, hey hi hello, now it's a World War. And please note: These escalations are driven by people, always by people—just as the escalation in your stories should be driven by characters, not by external events.

The most straightforward version of escalation occurs in *Die Hard*. We begin the movie with the tension of a man whose marriage is under siege going into a viper's nest of smarmy executives— and from there, it's just a layering of *bad thing* on top of *bad thing*. John McClane has victories, but those victories (in true storytelling form) do not de-escalate the tension—rather, they intensify the problem. Every victory McClane gains offers a new complication: He escapes, but he has no shoes; he gets a machine gun and, later, the detonators, but this only triggers a violent hunt to find him; he summons the police, but the police and the FBI only heighten tensions because they are either inept or overly aggressive. This goes on and on—the explosion McClane sets off early in the elevator shaft is clearly an escalation that deepens the tension because:

1. It's a literal explosion that does damage to the building and takes out terrorists.
2. It foreshadows what would happen if *all* those bombs were to go off, thus raising the stakes and hinting at the massive *boom* that arrives in the third act.
   and
3. It also tells us what stakes are on the table for the terrorists, because they desperately need those detonators—which means

they're going to come at McClane *all the harder* to retrieve them. His life is about to get a whole lot worse.

In that movie, the tension ratchets in a direct, exponential way. It's rung after rung of a ladder in the steady climb to the top—if only so it can throw Hans Gruber off to his death.

Now, on the other hand, let's take a peek at *The Empire Strikes Back*. In *ESB*, the escalation is not so clean an ascent. We begin with the tension of Luke and the Wampa, which escalates to Luke almost freezing to death, which escalates to a gigantic battle that unfolds on the icy mantle of Hoth. To go back to the *shape* of narrative, it shows a story that begins with a sharp rise to conflict—

And then it falls quickly from that peak.

Meaning, all that happens *in the first act*. It is arguably a story shape that would encompass an entire story, one that ends with a massive battle. But *ESB* gets the battle out of the way early. The fire that burns so bright is suddenly smothered, and we finally get a big gulp of oxygen. The movie slows down a bit. It focuses on the characters, on their relationships, and all the while, that oxygen primes the pump for *more* tension, not less. It draws the story out like a tightening cord—even though it's not all about big space battles, just the same, there's no slack in that rope.

It can do this in part because we already know these characters, so there's not a lot of time needed for introducing them and their problems. Here, we get Han and Leia on the asteroid, we get Luke training with Yoda, we get the gang converging upon Cloud City—and during this large expanse of the second act, we are still treated to spikes of tension releasing through action (space slug! escaping the Empire! Yoda is riding you like a monkey, young padawan, and doesn't think you're up to the task of being a real Jedi!), but those spikes never exactly rise to the level of the larger battle at the fore of the film.

But that's okay! Because *ESB* is playing with a different *kind* of escalation. Just because the escalation isn't as traditional as the escalation present in *Die Hard* (which is more physical in that the danger lies in the possibility of McClane's body being perforated by lots of bullets), that doesn't mean *ESB* isn't escalating—it just moves in a different, and more personal, direction.

(Speaking of different directions, it's worth again reminding ourselves of the image of a roller coaster: a three-dimensional ride that is sometimes about going up slowly, sometimes about going down swiftly, but other times about whipping right or left, corkscrewing through the air, or turning us upside down when we think we should be right-side up.)

The conflicts within *ESB* deepen and thicken like a good sauce on simmer—and we can start to see the transition from galactic conflict to the more meaningful one of interpersonal conflict. Yes, of course the film still gives us the standard physical threats—we get space fights and meteor slugs and R2 gurgling into the mire—but the escalation is in the movement of the characters. Han and Leia pinball off each other as romantic tension ratchets tighter, and Lando enters the picture as an agitating element (suave, shifty, you're not sure where he stands). Luke and Yoda seem perpendicular to one another, too—Luke's impatience clashes with Yoda's wisdom, and both of them doubt that this Skywalker kid can really pull off being a Jedi. All that comes to a head on Cloud City. Luke bails on the little gremlin to save his friends. Lando betrays them to Vader, and, as a result, Han gets turned into a coffee table. But these escalations are also revelations: Luke realizes that his friends are more important to him than his training, Leia realizes she's in love with Han, C-3PO realizes *he's* in love with R2-D2.[18] Those revelations are like the victories McClane experiences in *Die Hard*: They serve to

---

[18] SHOW ME THE LIE.

complicate their problems rather than eradicate them. They *add* to the maze rather than *subtract* from it.

And then comes the bunker buster bomb of the final duel between Luke and Vader, where Vader reveals the truth: that Obi-Wan is Luke's father because Obi-Wan had a scandalous affair with Padmé Amidala—

is handed a note

Okay, I am assured that's not how it goes.

Whatever.[19]

Point being: Though the actual ending is not as *physically* epic as the conclusion of the first act—given that there are no stompy AT-ATs or exploding shield generators—it is significantly more *emotionally* epic. The escalation is present, just with a different (and arguably more meaningful) emphasis. We have left the need for a showy ending behind and made it very much about the characters' own journeys. The stakes have not merely been raised, they've been transformed by these revelations. And it sets the stage for the final act of the original saga: *Return of the Jedi*, where an insurgency of slavering rat-bears helps bring down the Empire so that they can have a steady supply of canned food in the form of stormtroopers.[20]

Also in contrast to *Die Hard*, *ESB* lets the beats play out longer toward the end—the events don't come fast and furious. We are given far more oxygen than the fire consumes. Moments where Luke and Vader are stalking one another—or simply talking. Moments building up to Han dropped into a block of carbonite. Moments of rescuing Luke from the bottom of Cloud City. The film gives us these moments to create tension, not to rob it from us: It has not absolved the threat, for the sword of conflict still dangles over the proceedings, but when things slow down, we are given time to pause and consider the blade hanging above the characters' heads.

And, in a way, above our heads as an audience.

---

[19] My head-canon is firm on this.
[20] Again I say, SHOW ME THE LIE.

Because we don't want to see Luke hurt. We want Vader vanquished. We want them to rescue Han from his ice cube before the credits roll.

But we don't get *any* of that. Luke *is* hurt. Vader wins the duel, even as he loses Luke. They don't save Han—Han's gone, baby. The movie uses the slower, more ponderous moments at the end to ratchet tension tighter—

And then it never really lets it go. We end the film *still tense*. We exit it with questions, with fears, with grave uncertainty.

It's all in the arrangement. It's how you stack the elements, how much oxygen you pump in, how much fire will feed on all of it.

THE QUESTION MARK, THE PERIOD, AND THE EXCLAMATION: OR, THE POWER OF QUESTIONS AND THE DANGER OF ANSWERS

appears at your front door on a stormy night with a long, scraggly beard and a mad glint flashing in the eye

I COME FROM THE FUTURE WITH A DIRE WARNING.

I HAVE READ YOUR BOOK.

… OR RATHER I TRIED TO READ IT AND THEN PUT IT DOWN AND WENT TO DO SOMETHING ELSE.

BECAUSE IT WAS SUPERBORING.

YOUR BOOK WAS KILLED!

AND IT WAS EXPOSITION THAT DID IT! EXPOSITION MURDERED YOUR STORY! HEED MY WARNINGS! BEWARE EXP—oh hey, sorry, I had my caps lock stuck again.

What I'm trying to say is, exposition and backstory are, well, I hesitate to say they're *bad* or *wrong*, because they're not. They are useful tools when used appropriately, but *more* often, exposition and backstory are real roadblocks.

To understand why this is, we need to understand a bit more about traversing the geography of narrative and what we can do to speed up travel, slow it down, and lure the audience through the story like a witch promising candy to children.

Imagine, if you will, that a story can have a lot of geographical features, much as our world does. It has mountains and valleys, it has rivers and highways, it has tracts of city and empty fields, it has wide seas and dread deserts. And though no individual feature of your story's geography is inherently troublesome, some geographical features *are* easier to navigate than others.

A river will pull you along if you travel with it, or block you if you come to cross it. A highway, too, though man-made, is an avenue of movement. A mountain is an obstacle, but a dramatic and exciting one—jagged peaks and avalanches and probably yetis![21] A desert can have hidden beauty, but it can also be a long slog through unrelenting sands and in blistering heat. You can only take so much desert before needing a respite.

Some aspects of a story pull the audience along, accelerating them through the narrative. Other elements put on the brakes. They slow things down. (Remember fire and oxygen?)

Dialogue, for instance, tends to be a *lubricating* component. Dialogue greases us up like a wiggly pig and launches us down the chute. Dialogue is best when it's a slide, not a staircase. But the shape of dialogue matters. Faster, shorter bits of dialogue speed us up. Slower, more ponderous dialogue—expository dialogue in particular—slows us down. Exposition in general runs the risk of becoming the desert mentioned earlier—an unremitting tract of sand, a long slog through heat where the payoff for the audience is uncertain.

---

[21] "Probably Yetis" is the name of my new band. And, yes, I'm stealing this joke from renowned science fiction author John Scalzi, and if he wants it back he will have to fight me for it.

The shape of the story in general is like this, too—faster, punchier elements in a tighter arrangement are snappier, swifter, *whoosh*. But the more you bloat and bulge the tale, the slower it goes.

And that is *not automatically a bad thing*. As noted in my explanation of fire and oxygen, sometimes we *need* to slow the story down. *The Empire Strikes Back* slows down at the end because we need time to consider the weight of what's happening—it allows the physical and emotional dread of Darth Vader hunting Luke Skywalker to build and the revelation to hit us right in the gut.

But you want to do this willfully, with great purpose.

Exposition is less necessary than you might think. And, in practice, it often ends up feeling more like crossing the desert than hiking and climbing a beautiful mountain—it feels like a chore, a burden put upon the audience.

Here's why: Questions, like dialogue, move us through a narrative. The audience is a junkie, we as storytellers are the dealers, and our product is *mystery*. I'll say it again: The question mark is shaped like a hook for a reason. It drags us forward. It is like the rapids of a river or a mudslide down a mountain—we can't help but want to know *answers*.

Ah, but the opposite side of that is also true: Just as questions give the story forward momentum, answers to those questions halt that momentum. A question draws us in, and a period forces us to stop. This is literally true at the sentence construction level, isn't it? A joke works by asking us a question and making us want the punch line; the question mark is the lure of continuation, the tantalizing mystery to be unraveled. The answer or the punch line always comes with a period—and that's it. Game over, man. The journey has ended. The answer has completed the exchange. It's not the promise of a juicy hamburger on the plate: It's the ketchup-smeared apocalypse that remains. The burger is gone. We're full now, thanks.

Exposition is not a question.

Exposition is an answer.

Worse is when exposition provides an answer before we've even had the enticement of the question. Exposition is almost a spoiler incurred by the storyteller: Before we've had a chance to care about the mysteries present, the potential of those mysteries is already ruined by overdrawn explanation or backstory. Once again, it becomes clear:

Arrangement matters.

Exposition up front, before questions are asked or pondered, is like telling us at the fore of Star Wars that Luke and Leia are Darth Vader's kids. (Don't get me started on how prequels actually do this—in fact, prequel material to any story is often exactly this, exposition for the sake of exposition, only there to retroactively undercut mystery with a nonessential story, and usually, if I'm being cynical, made solely to make someone money.) It robs the chance of tantalizing the audience. It removes the seductive joy of mystery, of not knowing what's around the corner. It's like a haunted house where someone has already mapped out all the scary parts before you ever get in the door.

Never give the audience more information than they need to progress through the narrative. And by "more information," I mean explicit explanations via exposition. If we envision our narrative as a house and, to get to the next room, the audience needs a key to proceed, give them the key. And that's it. Stop there. You don't need to keep going. "Here's a key, and a burlap sack full of nickels, and a baby dragon, and by the way here's how the thermostat works, and the trash guy comes on Tuesday mornings, and wait hold up here's a copy of *Moby Dick*, let's read it together."

It's *okay* that the reader or viewer only has the key to get themselves to the next room. It's *perfectly awesome* that they don't know what to expect, or that they can look around this room and the next and have questions about what they see. Not everything needs to be explained, so don't give an explanation if they don't need one. And when an explanation is necessary, give them as little exposition as you can, as quickly as you can muster.

Exposition is about a thing that already happened. It's backstory about a person or a place—it's writ, it's wrought, it's done. You only need to go through exposition if *not* having that information will be confusing to the audience—or if you're performing some act of misdirection as per stage magic. (When Obi-Wan sits Luke down and is all like, "Luke, your Dad was a really cool dude who totally got killed by that shiny jerk, Darth Vader," that's a piece of information that 1) we need, and 2) is *misdirection.*[22])

Treat exposition like you're having sex with a swamp creature.[23] It's crass and shameful and should be done as hastily and as hurriedly as possible.

The *best* exposition is the kind that leaves us asking more questions.

Because, again, questions are everything.

Once upon a time, when I was a Baby Writer who thought he knew everything (as opposed to now, where I am a Petulant Adolescent Writer who thinks he knows *most* things), I said:

"Conflict is the food that feeds the reader."

Meaning, above all else, you need conflict.

And now, I'm going to disagree with myself—or, rather, I'm going to change my opinion just slightly:

"*Questions* are the food that feeds the reader."

Further, I'll note that conflict is just another question. What I mean is this: Imagine the simplest, most brutal form of conflict. Let's say it's just two characters bare-fistedly punching the king-hell out of each other. Whap, whomp, biff. A bloody, pugilistic brawl.

Why does that matter? Why does the brawl engage with us? Okay, ideally we'd have some sense of the characters—who they

---

[22] Once again I echo: "From a certain point of view." One might think that Obi-Wan was not only telling a half-truth there, but also giving us something to think about regarding how stories are told and who is doing the telling.
[23] Sorry, I shouldn't kink-shame.

are, what they want, why they're pounding the boogers out of each other—but even *without* that. Let's say we just flipped on the TV and saw two characters whaling the poop out of one another.

The very nature of that struggle is one of question. The outcome is uncertain. Who wins is unknown. The circumstances surrounding the fight are a question, too. And even when one character does win, that is a resolution that potentially leads to more questions— will the loser survive? Will the winner be a good winner, or will he kick the poor bastard when he's down? Did the fight resolve anything? Will a rematch occur? Is everyone even *okay*, what with all that blood and rage?

Conflict is in itself a form of question. Implicit in every conflict, in every breach of the status quo, are a bundle of uncertainties.

Will our hero persevere?

Will she conquer her demons or be herself conquered?

Will she live, will she die, will she love, will she cry?

Will she get her revenge, will she get a donut, will she get eaten by one of those insurgent rat-bears?

We just don't know.

And that's why conflict works.

Because, damnit, we want to know.

The question is one of your most fundamental building blocks— and key to the arrangement of your story.

THE MYSTERIOUS MISTS OF MYSTERY: OR, THE POWER OF QUESTION-DRIVEN PLOTTING

To repeat: Questions are the food that feeds the audience. Or, to be more precise: Answers feed the audience, and questions keep them hungry. And boy, howdy, do we want them hungry! We want them hungry enough that they keep coming back for another nibble—but we don't want them so mad with hunger that they put the book down or turn the show off. Storytelling is an act of delivering satisfaction in the most meager doses possible. It's a tightrope act—you don't want them overfed, you don't want them underfed. Always hungry, never starving.

Now, *plotting* a story—whether you outline it on paper or inside your own skull cave—is the act of moving the story forward, step by step and scene by scene. It is, loosely, the act of determining the sequence of events *as it is revealed to the audience*. Not just what happens when, but the arrangement of those events and how the revelations stack up. An outline becomes *this is revealed, then that, then this other thing, now the end*.

The problem is that, when we approach it this way, we run the risk of a disconnected, external plot taking over the narrative. Plot ends up being this giant, Godzilla-shaped, kaiju thing, grumpily staggering through the cityscape of your characters, stepping on everything and knocking shit down and carving its own cataclysmic swath through the careful architecture and urban planning you've created. We don't want that. We don't want *event*-driven plotting. We want *character*-driven plotting, where the agency of an individual character pushes and pulls against the agency of all the *other* characters. Then the story that's told is not so much a clean line as it is a web—tug here, feel it there—a constant balancing and rebalancing.

How do we get there? How can we plot and scheme that out? How do we take a ground-level, organic approach to plotting?

First we take LSD and wander naked into the jungle to find and fight the Jaguar King and then from there—

Wait, whoa, that's not right at all. I'm so sorry.[24]

No. What I mean to say is that we begin with questions.

Two kinds of overarching questions drive a story:

1. The questions that drive the characters.
2. The questions that drive the audience.

---

[24] I do not advocate hallucinogens or nudity in any combination to jump-start your narrative process. But also, I'm not *not* advocating it.

In one sense, the two are linked—the questions that drive the characters should also drive the audience. The reverse is not necessarily true: The questions that drive the audience are not necessarily the same ones that the characters need answers for, nor are they questions the characters may even be *aware* of. This is the power of dramatic irony, which is not irony as we (or Alanis Morissette) understand it, but rather a narrative conceit where the audience knows something the character doesn't. Dramatic irony again reveals the power of arrangement: We the audience know Who Murdered Dave even as Mary searches for the killer. We have been given information she has not, and so the suspense is less about the question of a murderer's identity and far more about when Mary will catch on and what will happen to her in her search for the answer. It's what I like to think of as the suspense of scuttlebutt: tension driven by our having unique information, as if we've heard a secret that we weren't meant to know. This happens to us in reality sometimes, right? We know that Steve cheated on Betty, but *Betty* doesn't know yet, and suddenly we're face-to-face with Betty and panic ensues. *Oh shit, omg, what does Betty know, does she suspect anything, what will happen when she finds out, will they get divorced, what will the kids do, will this break up the group of friends we have, will she cut off his head with hedge clippers and mount his skull on a flagpole?*

It's the suspense of having information but not yet knowing the consequences. We have an answer, but not an outcome.

More to the point, we have an answer that just created more questions.

And those are the best kinds of questions to ask: questions that generate more question marks than periods or even exclamations.

So! Back to it—two kinds of questions at the fore, *questions for the character* and *questions for the audience.*

Let's start with questions that drive the characters.

Character Questions

These are *small* story questions—they center upon the smaller story of the individuals that populate the tale. They are given over to the same necessities already laid out so far in the book: *What is the character's problem? How does that character intend to solve this problem?*

It begins almost like a game with pieces on a board. Or, if you're a superdorky dork face like me, a bit like a session of *Dungeons & Dragons*. You've got these characters existing independently from one another, and now they're about to intersect—so what happens? You're trying to *game* the narrative for maximum emotional impact, which means the journey of each character through the maze should meet the journey of every other character—they travel together (as noted, parallel) or intersect as foes (as noted, perpendicular), and a story unfolds. Imagine that you're writing *A New Hope.*

Luke Skywalker, in search of adventure and wanting to leave his boring sand-bucket planet, is trying and failing to convince his Aunt and Uncle to let him leave—and then here comes a pair of droids, who initially intersect with him at a perpendicular angle. They crash into his story, and they complicate it.

Luke meets the droids. His role is to keep them trapped (fitted with restraining bolts, remember). Their role is to find Obi-Wan.

Questions arise. How will the droids get to Obi-Wan? Answer: Artoo completely manipulates Luke. He plays a snidbit (snippet + tidbit) of Princess Leia's message, which leaves Luke with more questions. (Note: Artoo is totally playing the role of storyteller here by enticing Luke along.) And then Artoo promises more of the recording *only* if he can have his restraining bolt off. Luke takes it off, and Artoo still withholds the message. Which not only tantalizes Luke further, it also affords Artoo the chance to escape.

Like on a chessboard or in a roleplaying game, these characters have each tried to outmaneuver the other, sometimes willfully, other times unconsciously. Each gets a turn where we the storyteller can ask, how will the character pursue his goals in spite of obstacles and complications? Once Artoo escapes, we must ask: How will Luke respond? While obviously he could choose not to pursue, that would place Artoo's escape on *his* head. And we already know something very important about young Luke Skywalker, don't we?

He is in search of adventure.

And so he goes off in search of the escaped droid. He has given into adventure, which leads us to ask: What's out there? Will he find the droid? Is the droid destroyed or stolen? We've already established that the droid is looking for Obi-Wan (aka "Old Ben") Kenobi—who is that hermit, really? Will the droid find who he's looking for? It is also established that danger waits in the wilds of Tatooine in the form of barking Tusken Raiders—whose very name implies a quest of their own (they are raiders, so they want supplies or food or slaves). Their quest intersects with Luke's—violently, I might add—and then Obi-Wan appears, with his quest crashing into the intersection of Luke and the Tusken Raiders.

The narrative in fact grows *more* complicated with the introduction of Obi-Wan Kenobi. We know he exists because the story has introduced us to these questions: Who is Artoo looking for? Old Ben. Who is Old Ben? Some old hermit living outside of town. We don't know much more than that, but what answers we have are intriguing—and incomplete answers draw us in. Furthermore, it means when he does show up, he's not just some *deus ex machina*—a hand of god appearing out of nowhere to save our sand-crusted flyboy and his two dirt-caked droids. We already know he's out there, a part of the plot, a question waiting to be answered. So when he shows up, it's organic and expected, not random and unwarranted.

From there, the characters push and pull on each other in ways that agitate and move the story along. Plus, the characters are given questions—some we can intuit, some that are more boldly placed into the narrative—that drive them. Who is Luke's father? How will Han deal with the debt hanging over his head? Who is the princess, and how will Luke and Han rescue her? Each answer creates more questions and problems.

Put differently, every answer to every question—every solution to every problem—has consequences.

Questions have answers, and answers lead to more questions. These chain together, ultimately, into a story. And they chain together in a way that is consequential—meaning, they're not simply *this happens, then this, then this*, but rather, each effect is preceded by a cause.

Or, put differently:

An action taken by a character in pursuit of an answer and/or a solution has:

1. an opposite or perpendicular reaction ("but then!")
   and/or
2. a consequential or parallel action ("because of!")

Let's look back at Luke leaving his desert igloo to chase after the wayward droid into the badlands of Tatooine.

You could easily write that as: "Luke goes on a wild goose chase after a wandering droid and *because of that* is attacked by a pack of ugly Tusken Raiders, who live out in the fringes of the Tatooine desert. *But then* Luke is saved by Old Obi-Ben-Wan What's-His-Name, who also lives out there."

One thing leads to another. One action taken in pursuit of a goal or a question leads to another, not because the plot lines up that way ("*and* then"), but rather because of cause and effect—because of consequence.

Eventually, of course, a story draws to a conclusion. It has to end. And that's when you start introducing answers that don't create more questions. That happens because the characters are all closing in on their goals. They are close to solving their problems, often at the expense of (or in opposition to) one another. You don't want to let more snakes out of the can than you can kill, after all, lest the audience be left feeling unsatisfied and bereft of answers. (Though a story also needn't ever answer *all* the questions. It's good to leave a few outstanding … just to keep the audience's noodle turning after they close the book or the credits roll.)

Those are character-driven questions. They begin with individuals, then move to questions about relationships—how those relationships begin, evolve, and conflict in the form of drama.

What about audience-driven questions, though?

Audience Questions

These are questions that sort of … *linger* behind the scenes, that drive you, the storyteller, and that urge the audience onward, but that exist beyond the ken of the characters. These are *detail-driven* questions.

Audience-driven questions don't necessarily apply to the characters because the characters ostensibly already know—or just don't care about—the answers. A show like *Game of Thrones* or *Lost* or *Westworld* has a ton of world-building questions implicit: Some of them beg us to ask about an individual clue; others are more seamless and beg us to ask about the culture of dragons or how the robot hosts work or, wait, did I just see a polar bear? What does the polar bear eat? Is the polar bear friend to, or enemy of, the White Walker zombie horde? What are the sexual customs of the Polar Bear Kingdom? Am I mixing up my storyworlds again? Should I stop ruminating on the sexual customs of Polar Bear kings and queens? Probably, but so what, *you don't control me, reader.*

You also have *thematic* questions at play. Though we'll talk more about theme in a later chapter (poke, poke, keep reading, or just flip forward to the Theme chapter on page 178), the audience is subject to deeper questions. These questions might be, "What is the role of love in a harsh world?" "What does it take to turn a hero into a villain or vice versa?" "Why is Chuck still going on and on about the royal fornications of a Polar Bear Kingdom, and doesn't he know that's not even a thing? Why is he so weird? He's still eating that candy bar and staring at me, and I'm calling 9-1-1."

Audience-driven questions are not the bread-and-butter, meat-and-potatoes of your narrative—they cannot *sustain* it. And shows that try too hard to sustain that (looking at you, *Lost*) forget to place at the fore the questions that urge the characters to action. Just the same, they are worth your consideration, more as a flavor component rather than the part that delivers the most nutritive value.

THE SCREW AND THE NAIL: THE BUILDING BLOCKS OF FUN FICTION

Maybe you're wondering what *specific* moves are in your arsenal—certainly all these game metaphors, whether we're talking chess or *D&D*, could use some particulars. In chess, the knight can move in an L-shape. In *D&D*, a rogue gets bonuses to backstab.

What "moves" do your characters get inside a story?

More specifically, what strategies can you use to tweak the narrative, to up the stakes, to build investment in the story on the part of the audience?

Now, before we begin the list, know this: None of these should drop out of nowhere. *All* should have buildup—not be forced into the narrative like cramming a square peg in a round hole or, worse, like shoving a skunk through a mail slot. We are aiming for organic inclusion. Anytime we embrace one of these moves, we want to first ask three questions: Would a character really do that? Does it make sense? And is there evidence to support it?

Not to get all *intellectual*, but a story is like an academic paper. Each piece must be supported by and proven within the work. When a character decides to betray another, it can surprise us as audience members, but it must not violate what we believe about that character. It either has to be supported or even foreshadowed by the character's words and actions up until that point, *or* it has to make sense retroactively as the story goes on. These litmus tests are vital so as not to make the audience feel like the spurned, betrayed party.

What follows is a list of twists, tweaks, and tickles you can include to jab shock prods up the story's nether region (bzzt!) and move the characters along. These techniques are especially useful when you're in the long slog of the *mushy middle*, which is an easily preventable (or at least escapable) tract of septic swampland that could threaten to fill the middle chunk of your story, the one strung between an exciting beginning and a thrilling end. Some of these are directly character driven. Others serve more as narrative mechanics, but their use should remain organic and bound with the characters, their problems, their limitations, and their motivations. All are meant to create tension, build mystery, and energize the story. Use them well—stories are built from these kinds of moments.

The Building Blocks of Tension

- **ALLIANCE:** Two characters align. Easy peasy—this one is the bread-and-butter of fiction (genre fiction in particular). Frodo and Sam meet Aragorn. John McClane joins forces with Al Powell. Luke Skywalker grows a band of heroes and friends to go against the Empire. Sometimes, too, an alliance is about a previously perpendicular relationship turning parallel, like Aang the Avatar joining up with Prince Zuko to defeat the Fire Nation in *Avatar: The Last Airbender*.
- **BACKED INTO A CORNER:** A character forced into an unwinnable situation—trapped by circumstance or by the movements of other characters—becomes unpredictable and all the more interesting. (Consider the character of John Rambo, who in *First Blood* is a killing machine trained by the military and ends up on the lam from local police. When cornered, he digs in and becomes an insurgent soldier in his own land. His *entire story* is built off this building block.)

- **BETRAYAL OF ANOTHER:** Characters in pursuit of their own quest or problem may betray one another, and this adds tension. This can be selfish, like Han Solo bailing on Luke, Leia, and the Rebel Alliance at the end of *A New Hope*, or more dire, like when Harry Ellis decides to (try to) smarm Hans Gruber to save his own tail. It can also be a crescendo moment, one that is both physically and emotionally climactic, such as when Darth Vader goes pro wrestler on his master, Palpatine, tossing him into that giant space toilet, or whatever it was.

- **BETRAYAL OF ONESELF:** Characters are very, very good at screwing themselves over and standing in their own way. In fact, this is the primary mode of tragedy. We speak about tragedy in day-to-day life as if it's nothing more than a sad event—but in storytelling, tragedy is about a character accidentally orchestrating his own downfall. (Think Oedipus, Hamlet, Charlie Brown. Yes, that's right, *I just said "Charlie Brown."* Fight me.[25]) Anakin Skywalker in the prequels is a tragic figure who betrays himself—by trying to solve his problem, he actually triggers the problem instead. Anakin desires to save his love and the galaxy, and so he falls to the Dark Side in search of the power to protect everyone, and that fall helps him hurt (and kill) his lover *and* doom the galaxy to an autocratic rule under that wretched old goblin-man, Palpatine.

- **BETRAYAL OF WHOLE DAMN AUDIENCE:** Put differently, this is an unreliable narrator situation. Not to reveal too much, but eventually we learn who Tyler Durden in *Fight Club* and Keyser Söze in *The Usual Suspects* really are, and we realize that we (as the audience) were sold a lie. Both Durden and Söze are not what we believe them to be, and the very *reason* we have bad information is because of the narrator: the nameless protagonist in *Fight*

---

[25] Seriously, if you can think of Charlie Brown eternally going to kick a football that is yanked away from him and *not* consider that tragic, then we don't understand each other.

Club, and Verbal Kint in *The Usual Suspects*. Narrators can be unreliable because they are cunning or because they are cuckoo bananapants. Either way, they can betray the audience by dint of delivering bad narrative data.

- **BLOW THEIR DAMN MINDS:** That moment in a story when a character's entire paradigm shatters and their head practically explodes with new awareness of their situation? It's not just a twist for the sake of a twist; it's a twist because it very specifically targets a character's worldview (with the goal of curb-stomping it). Think when Neo learns the truth of *The Matrix*, or when Luke learns about Vader, or when Jon Arbuckle realizes that the orange cat, *Garfield*, has been a figment of his imagination this whole time.[26] Whoa, brain explodey!

- **CHANGE OF SETTING:** Changing location in the story keeps it fresh. Every narrative has the probable side benefit of introducing unfamiliar places, people, and situations, and a shift in setting exploits that benefit. The Star Wars movies tend to each visit three primary places—*ESB* shows us Hoth, Dagobah, and Cloud City, for instance—and each place is tied very explicitly to the plot and the characters. We start out on Hoth, Dagobah is the home of Yoda, and Cloud City is Lando's location. That means each location change is not simply for the sake of introducing a new place, but also to tie it to the journeys of our characters. The entirety of *Die Hard* is largely contained to Nakatomi Plaza and its surrounding environs, and so the change of setting comes when McClane works his way through its levels, from the executive suites to the unfinished floors to the various shafts and ducts.[27]

- **DECEPTION:** Lies are delicious cookies when it comes to the fictional food that feeds the audience. Lies hold power and cre-

---

[26] Okay, that's not actually a real thing, but it is one of the more interesting pop culture "fan-theories" out there.

[27] "Shafts and ducts" sounds oddly pornographic, and I apologize.

Damn Fine Story

ate tension when they are spoken (if we know them to be lies through the mechanism of dramatic irony), and they also create that tension when they are revealed as deception. Obi-Wan telling Luke stories about his father is a narrative we don't recognize as a lie until later. But when Loki—throughout mythology or in any Marvel comics property ever—says something, we assume it's a lie, and that gives his every word tension. Because we don't know. We don't know what's a lie, what he's hiding, what the consequences are. And it's perfectly emblematic of his character.

Now, a character shouldn't lie just to lie. It should be purposeful and within character, and by that I mean written within the character's spectrum of motivation, and not just to give the plot some pizazz.[28]

• **DIFFICULT (OR IMPOSSIBLE) CHOICE:** You might also call this "torn between two horses." Remember how we give characters problems? How they have wants and desires and fears? Pit them against each other. Force the character to make a choice—she really wants to SAVE HER HUSBAND and SAVE HER CHILD, but she can only do one. She really wants to KILL THE VAMPIRE or EAT THAT DELICIOUS HIPSTER DONUT SHE PAID LIKE TWELVE BUCKS FOR. Whatever. Point is, the character has competing desires, and inside the labyrinth of the story she has to make a choice to go left or go right. Can't do both. Tension is born. Need examples? Luke has a choice in *ESB* to continue his training or save his friends. The consequences of each are somewhat dire: If he keeps training, his friends may die. If he abandons his training, he may encounter Vader before he's ready, and *he* may then die or fall to the Dark Side.

A danger to this is when authors force a false choice—meaning, the character has other avenues, but the author forces the

---

[28] Do people still say "pizazz" anymore? I don't know if I've heard anyone say that word in years. I'm not sure *I've* said that word in years, even though I write it. I'm going to start saying it a lot now, and I hope you'll join me. Pizazz!

character not to see them. Anytime the audience feels smarter or more mature than the characters is not ideal, and if you're going to sell this kind of dichotomy, it has to be done for good reason. It either has to be logical or emotionally relevant. A logical choice means the audience won't see a third and obvious path you've chosen to neglect mentioning. An emotional choice means that the audience will accept a bad decision because that's who the character is—certainly, bad decisions are the bread-and-butter of fiction, and we don't want to keep those off the table. They just have to *make sense* for the character.

- **ESCALATION:** Characters may escalate tensions on their own for their own benefit or as an effort to solve a problem. I like to think of this as the *chaos reigns!* option, and it's one you see often enough when you're playing a tabletop role-playing game like *D&D*. Inevitably, one of the players decides to have their character do something completely batshit wacky—first because it solves a problem, and second because it complicates the story and makes things interesting. It's the "there's a rat in the house so I summon a demon to kill it" situation. It's a lot of fun, and it works well with certain kinds of characters. John McClane in *Die Hard* routinely takes a chaotic way of dealing with problems, which really only intensifies things: He blows up an elevator shaft, he throws a corpse out a window, he taunts the terrorists with bloody sweatshirt messages. He creates chaos as he solves problems, and *hot damn* is it fun to watch![29]

- **FALSE IDENTITY:** Fiction is brimming with false identities. Darth Vader! Tyler Durden! Verbal Kint! Sometimes it's that people are hiding and pretending to be someone they're not. Sometimes it's a case of mistaken identity, as in *The Wrong Man*, *The Big Lebowski*, and *North by Northwest*. As with a lie, the tension can come from us already knowing the person isn't who they claim or from the discovery of a true identity.

---

[29] Pizazz!

- **FALSE VICTORY:** Let's say it again: The storyteller's job is to be a jerk. You're a monster. You're not the audience's buddy. You literally have the job of dangling candy in front of them and then yanking it away—or worse, as in this instance, replacing the candy with a dead fish or a goat's eye or something else horrid. This has the *out of the frying pan and into the fire* component to it—a character thinks they've escaped danger or won some victory when, in reality, the reverse is true. They screwed up. Things are now worse. Smooth move, Ex-Lax. In *The Matrix*, Neo finds the Oracle, and not only does he not get satisfying answers from her, the trip is also a trap set by Cypher—some of the crew dies, and Morpheus sacrifices his freedom to allow Neo to escape. An upward beat turns sharply downward because the Wachowskis (sibling writer-directors of the movie) are brilliant monsters who know how to manipulate us. John McClane in *Die Hard* is constantly turning the tables on the terrorists—only for it to blow up in his face (often literally).

- **FAST-FORWARD:** Time leaps are less a narrative trick determined by characters and more by you, the storyteller, but they remain effective for suddenly launching ahead beyond audience expectations in certain types of stories. TV shows, comics, and novels are better at this than films because films have limited narrative landscape in which to work, and you'll see it in *Battlestar Galactica*, *Lost*, even *Parks and Recreation*.[30] First, this serves to destabilize the audience—they thought they were on safe ground, and now they're not. The audience learns not to trust you, the storyteller, and that is a natural and necessary source of tension—the tension between the teller of the story and its recipient.

- **GOOD CHARACTER, BAD DECISION:** Suspense is created when a character we love makes a decision (or takes an action) that we hate. Buffy Summers gives Angel a moment of bliss and later has to banish the Evil Angelus—and we *hate* that, even though

---

[30] Aka, the greatest sitcom of all time, don't you dare disagree with me.

she had no other choice. When John McClane gives Hans Gruber a gun because he thinks Gruber is really an escaped hostage, we cringe—though, of course, McClane has a secret plan of his own there, doesn't he? The bad decisions characters make expose them to danger, and so it fosters tension in the audience.

- **GOT DEAD, OOPS:** Have you ever known anyone who has died? A friend, a family member, a public figure? George R.R. Martin killed them. He hunted them down and ended their story because that's the kind of monster he is, the kind of monster that kills characters. He is Death Personified. One day you, too, will die, and as you pass from this realm to the next, the man ushering you beyond the veil will be George R.R. Martin. What I'm trying to say is that it is a perfectly viable move to kill off a character, and it does indeed increase tension—and, further, it can engender surprise when you kill off a *main* character, like, say, Ned Stark in *A Game of Thrones*. That tells you the storyteller is serious business and not to be trusted.

  One caveat, though: Killing characters just for the sake of doing it starts to feel exploitative over time. It might be apropos for horror films, but too much of it and the audience will become aware of the storyteller actively trying to mess with them instead of responding to the death as a natural and organic part of the unfolding story. It's the difference between death as a consequence of choices made and death JUST BECAUSE IT'S PLOT-TASTIC FUN. You're a monster, not a sadist. Further, sometimes leaving a character alive creates more interesting consequences and implications than offing them.

- **GOT HURT, OW:** Pain is a powerful source of tension. Hurt a character, and if we care about that character, we get worried. John McClane is put through the ringer in *Die Hard*. So is Martin Riggs in *Lethal Weapon*. If we've done our job well and the audience cares about the character, then they will care about the character getting hurt. They want the character to *not* be hurt, and so it's your job to create that tension. Note, though, that causing them physical pain has to be a thing that comes prepackaged with ramifications for that character: The pain is not just set dressing. It's not cosmetic. When John McClane gets hurt, it's clear that he's hobbled.

- **LOVE, TWOO WUV:** Love is a powerful source of tension and an essential building block of fiction. Because we know, soon as you mash up two characters and make them go kissy-kissy woogy-woogy, then it becomes part of the stakes. It's part of the pool of chips in the middle of the poker table, and we know that it can be *lost*.

  Love provides us a variety of options for creating suspense. First up is the very popular *will-they-won't-they* component, where two characters skirt around the idea of falling in love but circumstances keep them from doing so, and the audience keeps biting their lip hoping it's going to happen. Then there's the *love triangle* maneuver—or the trickier-to-pull-off move, the love *rhombus*—where multiple characters push and pull on each other romantically, emotionally, and sexually, so the audience doesn't know who will end up with whom. Finally, you've got the *fear of shattered love*, where two people meet and fall in love, and now the audience is just waiting for the giant boulder above their heads to come crashing down and either kill one of them or at least separate them and end the relationship. A film that has a version of all three of these sources of tension is the masterful *The Princess Bride*, by the way. Go watch it right now. Never *don't* watch that movie when you have the chance.

- **MISDIRECTION:** Misdirection is something we always do as storytellers, admittedly, but it's also something that can be a literal part of the story that's unfolding. Think about how murder mysteries and heist films routinely try to get you to believe that so-and-so is the real killer, or how they keep certain parts of the heist plan hidden from view. The best example of this is the novel *and* the film *The Prestige*, which is about stage magicians competing against one another. The story brims with characters misdirecting one another, *and* the storytellers misdirecting *you*. It is a brilliant head screw and also a film that perhaps serves as the best metaphor for storytelling I've ever seen—the events that unfold as part of the plot also nicely represent what it is to be a storyteller.

- **MISUNDERSTANDING:** Misunderstandings are the cornerstone of sitcoms—and pretty much any movie starring Ben Stiller. The awkwardness with which two characters fail to grasp what the other is doing or saying leads to comedy, and comedy is sometimes a form of tension: A joke leads us to feel shocked, awed, bewildered, wondering what hilarious or absurd thing will happen next. *Seinfeld* and *Friends* are two good examples of shows that reveled in misunderstandings.

- **PROBLEM SOLVED, NOW WHAT:** A favorite narrative move of mine is to give the characters what they want, early. You establish a problem, you give off clues as to where the story is going by its end, and then you give the audience that solution—that climax—early on. When you do this, the audience is left reeling—they thought that the moment you just gave them at the midpoint was going to take the whole story. And now that the moment has come and gone, they're cast adrift. The audience expectations must be rearranged and reconfigured, and that's true of the characters, too. This occurs in *The Matrix*. Neo's initial struggle is just to find out what the Matrix actually is … and though it's something you would expect to take the entire movie to resolve, he learns the truth well before the midpoint of the movie.

  Television shows and comic books are also particularly good at this—it's more essential, in fact, to the narrative model of the genre. You don't know how many seasons or issues you're going to get, so you build in arcs and quests that conclude as they go, a constant rise and fall of plots and problems. A show that does this *very* well is *Orphan Black*, which is about a young woman who discovers she is one of several clones. It has mysteries packed into it similar to, say, *Lost*, but unlike that show, it doesn't waste its time in delivering answers. In fact, *Orphan Black* routinely answers big questions and solves problems while simultaneously using those solutions and answers to up the stakes further and create more dramatic tension.

- **REVERSAL OF CIRCUMSTANCES:** The technical definition of *peripeteia* in Greek tragedy is exactly this: when a character's circumstances change to their opposite. A character who had everything loses everything, or a character who had nothing gains everything. A character who hunts vampires becomes a vampire, or a character who is allergic to bees is filled with bees and becomes the Bee Queen of Sacramento. Or something. The most on-the-nose example of this would be *Trading Places*, where the rich and the poor (Dan Ackroyd and Eddie Murphy, respectively), um, well, trade places. Angel in *Buffy the Vampire Slayer* reverses his circumstances at least once every fifteen minutes, bouncing between Evil Angelus and Good Angel. Spike does it, too, though with far less magical enforcement, and Willow *also* does it and—wow, that's actually a cornerstone of the show, isn't it?

- **ROOSTING CHICKENS:** You have *surely* heard the phrase "the chickens come home to roost," yes? It's an idiom that suggests, very simply, that your actions will have consequences. Negative ones, ostensibly, as the phrase is never used to indicate something *good*—it's instead suggesting that karmic retribution is one of the constant laws of the universe. (Though why this is framed as your chickens coming home is beyond me. One suspects that if you have lost chickens, the best thing that can happen is that they come home to roost. Unless we're talking about demon chickens? That *would* be bad, I suppose.) A more realistic, though perhaps more crass, version of this would be, "That's going to come back and bite you on the ass."

Utilizing this particular building block in a story is not just about using the moment the metaphorical chickens come home, but also about how you build to that moment, because the audience tends to sense when *comeuppance* is on the menu. Storytellers pack in foreshadowing to essentially "warn" of the coming chickenpocalypse, and audiences pick up on those clues, and tension is created as a result. (Science fiction handles this particularly well—think *Frankenstein*, or *The Fly*, or time-travel films like *Primer*, *Looper*, or even *Back to the Future*. Characters routinely use or misuse technology for their own purposes and end up causing more harm than good. And then the story is either about playing this out or fixing the error.)

- **SACRIFICE:** A character's sacrifice—meaning they give up something vital and valuable, even as important as their own *life*—is a huge, pivotal moment that plucks at our heartstrings and reveals a special nobility in the character in question (or perhaps a gifted, savvy malevolence!). Obviously then the most classic version of this is Darth Vader at the end of *Return of the Jedi*—he sacrifices his role in the galaxy, and ultimately his own life, to save his son and, further, to reveal his own virtue. This might be more common than you think: *Terminator 2: Judgment Day*, *Mad Max: Fury Road*, *Independence Day*, *Titanic*, *Gran Torino*, *Aliens*, *V For Vendetta*, *Armageddon*, *Big Hero 6*, *Guardians of the Galaxy* ... and really I could do this for about two, maybe three more pages.

  Another version is when a character sacrifices his or herself, but the sacrifice doesn't really "take"—meaning, they don't actually go away. Look at Iron Man/Tony Stark in *The Avengers*, or Batman/Bruce Wayne at the end of the *The Dark Knight Rises*. Even some of the examples above play out that way. This is definitely a trope within comics and comic-based films, because in comics, characters are *constantly* dying and returning—or just failing to really die in the first damn place. It can become a little lazy, so the key is to either make it stick, to find a new spin on it, or to give the moment genuine consequence. A character who returns from the brink but isn't actually dead should bring baggage with him—and, arguably, in the Marvel films, Tony Stark definitely accumulates some emotional baggage. He is a character who starts to change in those films, which is a welcome shift from how we usually treat comic book heroes.

- **SECRETS EXPOSED:** Part of the narrative bedrock is the expectation that characters withhold information from each other. Tension is created because we know this to be true, and when we receive hints of secrets, we're engaged even more because we wonder: What is the truth, and when will it be revealed? Certainly I've kept secrets from you, dear readers. I have not told you, for instance, that I am the love child of Stephen King and Chuck Palahniuk,[31] created in a lab underneath the city of Seattle. Wait, I just told you the secret, didn't I? Damnit. PRETEND YOU DIDN'T READ THAT. Ahem. Anyway! In the Star Wars trilogy, both Obi-Wan and Yoda know secrets about the Skywalker heritage that they do not share with Luke. The show *Lost* uses this initially to great mastery—all of the characters have a cabinet of secrets that are revealed in portions to us through flashbacks, and then revealed differently to the other characters, and, for the most part, it works. When it *does* fail there (and could fail in your own story), it's because a character keeps a secret more to preserve a plot point than to preserve the integrity of her own character. When we, the audience, detect that the secret kept has been forced, it leaves a sour taste in our mouth, like we're sucking on an old sock.

- **SECRET PLAN ALL ALONG:** Frequently this is a villainous thing— like when a villain reveals, *ha ha ha, this has been my plan all*

---

[31] Though many also suspect I am the genetic hybrid of Alton Brown and the two Mythbusters (Jamie Hyneman and Adam Savage). The real story is that I am a bag of tarantulas.

along, but it works for heroes, too, at times. A bad execution of this occurs in *Skyfall*, the James Bond film, when villain Raoul Silva confirms that "being captured" was really his plan all along—but the execution of that doesn't hold up to scrutiny and requires such precision and luck that to accept it is to also accept that Raoul Silva is an actual fucking wizard. Maybe he's Voldemort? I don't know. A *good* example occurs in *The Princess Bride* because we get both the hero and villain version. At the fore, we see how the Man in Black turns the tables on the egotistical Vizzini when he puts poison in *both* cups, but we also see how Prince Humperdink arranged the whole kidnapping-and-murder of Buttercup to start a war.

• **SEXY TIMES:** In real life, sex often releases tension, but in storytelling, it tends to *create* it. Why is that, exactly? Because sex complicates the story. Characters often think they can make the beast with two backs and it won't change them, but it does. Or they think they can do the ol' rumpy-pumpy without falling in love or growing jealous ... but oops, yeah, no, sorry. *Or* they expect that they can do the Lubrication Tango and that nobody will catch them in this forbidden act, especially not their loved ones, but eeek, ooooh, they're going to find out, because that's how stories work. More to the point, sex itself has a narrative swoop to it—a beginning, a middle, an end[32]—and, in storytelling, it is often part of a larger story. Sex always has a story, and it always *shapes* the story, in part because we shouldn't put pieces into the narrative that don't *affect* the narrative. Sex in the film *Juno* leads to a baby for the teen protagonist. Sex in horror movies often invokes a kind of moral and mortal trigger—there exists an unspoken and practically puritanical rule that to have sex in one of those films is to invite and even *deserve* death by the monster. Nearly every movie about an affair—from *Fatal Attraction* to *Brokeback Mountain*—is not just about the love and

---

[32] ahem

the romance, but about how sex confirms those things and is the trigger for consequence.

The great thing about sex as a driver of tension is that so many outcomes are possible: love, jealousy, pregnancy, awkwardness, breakups, murder, stains, trapeze acts, clown paint, various squishing noises, inadvertent arousal on public transportation ... okay, you get the point. But the larger thing to remember is that sex is not there to titillate the audience—sure, it can have that as a side effect. But it's ultimately about character, and about the tension of what happens when you *smush* these two characters (or three, or five, or whatever orgy you have in mind) into sexy-sexy times.

- **TABOOS AND TRANSGRESSIONS:** Related to the above is when a character breaks an understood taboo, engaging in a transgression that we suspect will have consequences. *Fifty Shades of Grey* is an example—though BSDM erotica is full of far better, if less well-known, instances—of a character's journey through sexual taboos. We expect that it will change her and affect her life in ways uncertain, and uncertainty breeds tension. Horror is full of taboo breaking, too: the cannibalism in *Ravenous*, the body horror of David Cronenberg's films, the dinosaur creation and act of playing god intrinsic to *Jurassic Park* (which, yes, is a creature-feature horror movie). Even Star Wars has at its core a transgression: The Jedi order is dead, and study of that ancient religion is forbidden, and so when Luke Skywalker undertakes his quest to become a Jedi, we know it's an act against the Imperial order. Superhero stories are often about breaking taboos— don't go there, don't do that, don't touch that, don't eat that, and then a character *does*, and becomes changed and superhuman as a result. Normal humans enter forbidden spaces and cease to be normal as a result. Cyberpunk fiction—really, *any* subgenre with *punk* in its name—often relies on going against the laws and norms of the social order, rebelling, and resisting to solve a problem.

- **TELL THEM THE ODDS:** This is a small but vital thing: If characters are up against danger, it helps to inform the audience just how bad that danger is, and just how unlikely it is for the characters to triumph (or even survive). You can do this as a setting background detail or, more common, through one of the characters in the story—C-3P0, for instance, is famous for rattling off the odds, often at the worst possible time. (Which leads to Han Solo's famous line: "Never tell me the odds.") The movie *300* (also a graphic novel) has the odds *right there in the title*.

- **TICKING CLOCK:** The ticking clock is a classic. OMG THE BOMB IS GOING TO GO OFF.[33] OH NO, THEY'RE GOING TO BLOW UP THE WORLD IN TWENTY-FOUR HOURS IF WE DON'T PAY THE RANSOM. IF WE DON'T DO THE THING BY SO-AND-SO TIME, THE BAD STUFF WILL HAPPEN. Look at *Back to the Future*, which uses a literal clock tower to mark the countdown to when Doc Brown has to utilize a single

---

[33] "There is a distinct difference between 'suspense' and 'surprise,' and yet many pictures continually confuse the two. I'll explain what I mean.

We are now having a very innocent little chat. Let's suppose that there is a bomb underneath this table between us. Nothing happens, and then all of a sudden, 'Boom!' There is an explosion. The public is surprised, but prior to this surprise, it has seen an absolutely ordinary scene, of no special consequence. Now, let us take a suspense situation. The bomb is underneath the table and the public knows it, probably because they have seen the anarchist place it there. The public is aware the bomb is going to explode at one o'clock, and there is a clock in the decor. The public can see that it is a quarter to one. In these conditions, the same innocuous conversation becomes fascinating because the public is participating in the scene. The audience is longing to warn the characters on the screen: 'You shouldn't be talking about such trivial matters. There is a bomb beneath you and it is about to explode!'

In the first case we have given the public fifteen seconds of surprise at the moment of the explosion. In the second we have provided them with fifteen minutes of suspense. The conclusion is that whenever possible the public must be informed. Except when the surprise is a twist, that is, when the unexpected ending is, in itself, the highlight of the story."

—Alfred Hitchcock

lightning strike (ironically hitting the very same clock tower) to help transport Marty back to the (wait for it) future.

- **VIOLENCE, SWEET VIOLENCE:** Characters fight. It is part and parcel to most genre fiction, and further, you'll find it in comedies, dramas, everything. (The puritanical component of American storytelling often sidelines sex in favor of violence, oddly.) Violence is the most blunt form of conflict and tension you can create: Implicit in any fight or battle scene/sequence is the question of who will win, who will lose, and what the consequences of that outcome will be. (We talk more about fight scenes on page 168 of this book.)

  The worst type of violence is when a fight scene is inserted just to have one: It's a false way of creating tension or delaying storytelling. Every fight should be tied to the problems the characters have. Every fight should have stakes on the table. Something to be won, something to be lost. A fight scene isn't *just* about putting an obstacle in the character's way—and that's because other characters are not obstacles. Remember: Characters are not architecture, but rather, architects. They fight for love, for jealousy, for hate, for revenge. Good examples of fight scenes? Those in *The Princess Bride* are loaded for bear with meaning, dialogue, and character beats. The entire Star Wars saga does them well, too, and even the most threadbare stormtrooper attack serves as a reminder of the oppression existing at every turn in the galaxy. Every fight in *Die Hard* has the stakes packed into it—and so do the ones in *Buffy the Vampire Slayer* because, tee-hee, stakes. Get it? Stakes? Because stakes hurt vampires?[34]

- **WE MIGHT LOSE:** There comes a moment in many stories where the characters must face the facts: *We're going to lose.* Whatever was to be gained will instead be lost. Whatever problem one hoped would be solved is now not only solved, but probably a lot worse. At the end of *A New Hope*, every X-wing run on the

---

[34] SHUT UP, THAT WAS A GOOD JOKE, DON'T YOU JUDGE ME.

Death Star fails again and again—and this is amped up at the end of *Return of the Jedi* when we learn the rebels have been drawn into a trap. In *Die Hard*, we routinely watch John McClane run out of options—up until the very end, when he's bloodied and out of (almost) all his bullets and Gruber has Holly. But this is about eking out a victory, scraping free from the narrow channel of Scylla and Charybdis[35] to snatch a win from the slavering jaws of defeat.

- **WE TOTALLY LOST:** On the other hand, sometimes the heroes *don't* get that win. Sometimes they lose. They have lost everything, or damn near to it. This can happen at any point in the story, really, though usually it is either a pivotal moment at the midpoint or a frame for the climactic ending. The end of *The Empire Strikes Back* shows Luke defeated, Han taken away, and Darth Vader mostly triumphant. We know Luke is the son of the tyrant, that the rebel alliance is in danger, and that everything they've worked for is now in question. The good guys *lose*. Now, that works because we know there's another movie coming, and it serves as one part of a larger story—so even though it serves as the climax of that one film, it also serves as the *midpoint* of the overall saga, thus showing how each building block of a story has its own narrative arc and can connect to a larger story. *Ghostbusters* (the original in particular) has this major defeat come as a lead-in to the final climactic act. All the ghosts are removed from containment, Dana is possessed, the city has gone to Hell, and all they've worked for is in ruins. This motivates them to act.
- **WE WON, BUT:** Ah, the Pyrrhic Victory—aka, We Won, But It Cost Us A Lot, So Did We Really Win At All? This is when the characters technically solve their problem and end their quest, but in doing so, have been so hurt or have done such damage

---

[35] Scylla and Charybdis are, mythologically, two sea monsters near one another—the first personified as a rock against which ships would crash, the other as a whirlpool that would swallow ships whole. Hence, traveling between them was a perilous journey with a very bad death near on both sides.

Damn Fine Story

that the victory is at *best* a complicated one and at worst is totally hollow. Consider the monumental costs and changes to the characters in *The Lord of the Rings*. The world is saved, but the characters are transformed—and not always in the best way. Or again we might look at *Ghostbusters*—sure, it's a comedy, but think about it. At the end of the movie, the ghosts are still free, a whole city block is ruined, and everything is a giant marshmallow mess. It's silly, and that's probably part of what makes it so fun—but the win was a rough one. So, too, with *The Avengers* or, really, most superhero movies that end with *most of a city left in ruins*. If you want a more somber, sober version, *Saving Private Ryan* is a great example of a film where the goals of the characters are ostensibly completed (they save the titular[36] Private Ryan), but given all they sacrifice to accomplish that—well, it's a victory whose cost is so high it's hard to see exactly how it's worth it. Not that "worth it" is the point of that story, to be clear, but it does neatly illustrate a Pyrrhic victory.

MORE TENSION TALK TO TITILLATE AND TERRIFY

Let's back away from the individual building blocks and once again resume the 30,000-foot view. What, exactly, is tension?

And how exactly do we cause it?

Tension and suspense, at the barest level, are the intermingled emotions of excitement and fear that come from uncertainty. We don't know what's going to happen, or why something is happening, or what it means, and so we feel that dueling sense of anticipation and apprehension. And we have lots of ways to create suspense and tension, as detailed above.

But at the heart of it all lies a greater, deeper source of tension.

---

[36] I'm not proud, but I giggle every time I say this word.

And that is the tension that exists between the teller of the story and its listener. It's in the antagonistic relationship between writer and reader, between filmmaker and viewer, between game designer and player.

The audience must never truly be sure of whether or not to trust you. They can't *hate* you, of course—not the whole time—but even *that* is a source of tension. Look at it this way: If every day you walk to work, and every day a guy jumps out of the bushes at the same spot and hits you with a shovel, that creates tension in the short term because, okay, you know that here it comes, here comes ol' Shovelface to give you a hard *whonnnng* to the chopper. But over time, that diminishes because the uncertainty has turned to certainty. You can plan for it. You can avoid it. You can be ready.

Ah, but now imagine that one day he hits you with a shovel, and the next he gives you a hundred bucks. And then a hundred bucks the day after that, and the day after that he hits you with a shovel again. There's no pattern. It's random. Day after day, either money or shovel, shovel or money, and you never really know which is coming.

Storytelling is like that. You're not there to *hurt* the audience, but you're not there to help them, either. Or, rather, you're there to do both. It's your job to mess with their expectations. You're there to surprise, to delight, to disturb. To hurt and to heal. You give characters some victories, and then you deliver them some staggering losses. Sometimes you reward them or upset them in ways they didn't even know they wanted, and other times it's your job to hand the audience exactly what they expect. Sometimes you're predictable—remember, the first few days of getting hit with the shovel are still tense *precisely because you know what's coming*—and sometimes you're unpredictable, because eventually you have to mix it up and stop giving them the same thing over and over again. With one hand you strike, with the other you soothe.

Tension is created by showing the sword dangling overhead, and when the audience demands to know about it, you just shrug. "Who knows?" you say. "Maybe it'll fall, maybe it won't. It probably will. But we don't know when." And then you show the sword drifting lazily. You show the fraying ropes holding it up. But the suspense isn't in the fall. It's in all the moments before.

To go back to the game metaphor from before, there exists a component of storytelling where it is you and the reader (or viewer, or whoever) sitting on opposite sides of a chessboard. You're always trying to outwit each other. And sometimes you need *them* to outwit *you*—the audience needs that power, needs to be invested. They want to do work, and they want (sometimes) to be victorious. Other times, they want the shock of loss, the joy at being outplayed. And at those times you misdirect and distract, and as they're thinking you're moving your piece one way, you move it another and shock them with your prowess.

But the trick is making all of this organic. It has to unfold naturally from the story—it's not JUST you screwing with them. It's you fucking with them within a framework that you built and agreed upon, a framework you've shown them, a place of rules and decorum. In this context, consider the game space. Like, say, a chessboard, or a *D&D* dungeon. The game space is an agreed-upon demesne. It has rules. It has squares. Each piece or character moves accordingly within those squares. It has a framework that everyone who has played the game understands.

And yet, the outcome is never decided. The game is forever uncertain even within established parameters. Surprises occur. You might win. Maybe I win. That's how storytelling operates best—we set up rules and a storyworld and characters, and you try to guess what we're going to do with them. We as storytellers shouldn't ever break the rules. Note: Breaking the rules in this context might mean conveniently leaving out a crucial storyworld rule

("Oh, vampires don't have to drink blood; they can drink Kool-Aid"), or solving a mystery with a killer who the audience couldn't ever have guessed ("It was the sheriff from two towns over who we have never before discussed or even mentioned"), or invoking a *deus ex machina* ("Don't worry, giant eagles will save them. It's cool"). You can still have chaos and uncertainty within the parameters—creating a framework, like building a house, doesn't mean it cannot contain secrets and surprises—but you stay within the parameters that *you created*.

Again, it's why *stage magic* works as a metaphor when *actual wizard magic* does not. With stage magic—tricks and illusions!—you can't really violate the laws of reality. But it damn sure *feels* like you do. Stories make you believe in wizard magic, but really it's just a clever, artful trick. The storyworld is bent and twisted, but never broken.

And, of course, your greatest touchstone for all of this is the characters, and their problems and places inside the storyworld.

The characters will forever be your guide, if you let them. They are the tug-of-war rope, the chess pieces, the *D&D* characters that exist as a connection between you and the audience. They are your glorious leverage.

SIDE TRIP TO TROPETOWN

Tropes. Know what they are? You don't? What's that? It's *my* job to explain it? UGH GOD, FINE.

In storytelling, we have identified and continue to identify certain patterns and motifs within the narrative. This is especially true of pop fiction, which often relies upon tropes, or recurrent themes, the way a man with a broken leg relies upon a crutch. Your greatest online receptacle for these is TVTropes.org, which offers these patterns in great detail, across a wide variety of stories, genres, and media. You know how in slasher films, the slasher killer always gets up one last time even though you think he's dead? Trope. You know how action movie characters say some glib shit before exploding the bad guy? Trope. You know how the bad guy will often explain his plan in needless detail to the hero, or how heroes always fall off buildings and land safely in dumpsters, or how a shotgun will blast a foe ten feet back and into some drywall with impossible (like, literally impossible) momentum? Tropity-trope-tropey-trope.

Tropes are not *universally* bad, even though using them runs the risk of you relying on lazy storytelling techniques. You can use them to your advantage, too. If you take individual tropes and twist them, or use them in unexpected ways, you can surprise the audience. The audience has unconscious expectations—even if they're not properly aware of tropes *as a thing*, they still can sense narrative patterns they've internalized. They expect the bad guy to give his villainous monologue. They expect that the handsome guy played by the popular actor is the hero. They expect dads to be dumb, nerds to wear glasses, that people who we don't see die on the screen or on the page are probably not really dead at all.

Here's a way to look at it: Tropes (and to a degree, character archetypes, too) are not single dots on a line, but rather, are lines themselves. Bent lines, bowed into arcs—meaning that they have a beginning and an end. Or, put differently, a trope has a *set-up* and a *resolution*. The storyteller sets up the trope—like Babe Ruth pointing where he's going to hit the homerun ball—and then completes it. The completion of the trope fulfills it and, further, fulfills the expectation. Problem is, there's no surprise there. Ah, but this is where you, the storyteller, can perform a *cool stunt maneuver*. You can begin the setup of the trope—and then go somewhere differently in the conclusion. You can point to the stands like Babe Ruth, and then when the pitch comes, you smack the bat and drive the ball right into the pitcher's crotch instead of way past the outfield.

Examples:

- The bad guy explains nothing and commences right to the torture.
- Or the bad guy tells his plan, but it's a lie—a carefully-constructed one meant to misguide the hero, and further, to misguide the audience.
- Or maybe the handsome hero guy in the story gets eaten by a bear in the first act.
- The dad isn't dumb, the nerds don't wear glasses and are the popular kids at this school, and the dead guy is totally dead.

That last one is a good example, actually, because, let's say you're writing a murder mystery, and early on an important character dies offscreen/off-page—you can drop false hints about that person not only being alive, but also being the killer. Of course, it's not true—but you can turn the audience's expectations against them.

One note, though: Some tropes are generally toxic and should be avoided at all costs (unless you *really* know how to turn them on their ear). Any trope that relies on shitty social messaging is one to cause worry. You know how MANLY MEN HEROES are often made to feel sad and spurred to action by a DEAD WOMAN? That's an overused pattern (called "Fridging," thanks to brilliant comics writer Gail Simone of the blog *Women in Refrigerators*) that relies upon the woman character having no agency and just being a prop to motivate the MANLY MAN'S MAN PAIN. You know that other thing, where you see a black character in an ensemble and you know that he'll be the first to die? Yep. Crappy. Don't do those things. Avoid them. And it's easily solvable by giving all characters agency and treating them like complete individuals with their own problems, motivations, questions, quests, and the like.

CHEKHOV'S ECHO

Heard of Chekhov's gun? It's a principle put forth by Anton Chekhov, playwright and short story writer, where he says: "If you say in the first chapter that there is a rifle hanging on the wall, in the second or third chapter it absolutely must go off. If it's not going to be fired, it shouldn't be hanging there." Some variations of it are about putting the gun on stage, giving it a theatrical bent. Either way, the point is the same: Something that appears now must appear again—no piece exists on its own, no piece is independent from the next.

Translation: A story is not just a string of connected bits all lined up in a row. It's not merely a sequence of events. It's a series of *echoes*. Characters do things and say things, and this creates consequences. Elements and objects appear, and they have weight and meaning inside the story. There are causes, and there are effects. Each piece is a rock thrown into the water, and the story is about the ripples—and how ripples reach the shore.

What Chekhov is saying isn't about a gun—he's saying the inclusion of a gun, *or any element*, must return. The echo must be heard throughout the piece. The gun is here now, so later it'll come into play again—likely when it goes off and probably shoots someone because, as it turns out, that's what guns are very good at doing.

In *Die Hard*, think about the scene where Gruber and the Beautiful Blonde German shoot out the windows so that McClane has to run barefoot across a floor glittering with shattered glass. Now, think about how that moment echoes up at the front of the story: McClane is tense from a plane trip, so he learns a lesson to ball up his toes and press them into carpet, which he does when he finally arrives at the party—and *boom*, that's when the terrorists arrive, and he doesn't have time to get his shoes back on. Then, throughout the story, he's *actively looking for shoes*. And he can't find them. (He even makes a comment about every dead terrorist having feet like his sister.) The storytellers constantly remind us of this single, seemingly unimportant thing: no shoes, barefoot, no shoes, barefoot, until that crucial moment late in the film when he has to run across glass. They don't just have him lose his shoes one minute and then run across glass the next; it's a moment that's been telegraphed early. The moments all echo into each other—ripples upon ripples, cause and effect, truth and consequence. It's small, and it's silly, but it's beautiful when all the pieces like that feel utterly intentional, like they feed each other and were not just throwaway moments.

Find the moments that echo. If they don't echo, you must either make them or you must silence them. No piece of your story is an island.

ABC: PLOTS AND SUBPLOTS AND SUB-SUBPLOTS

The arrangement of a narrative is often singular in its focus: It details the peaks and valleys, dips and pivots, of a single story. But a single story needn't be such a direct thrust. Imagine the metaphor of a roller coaster, but now weave in *another* roller coaster—perhaps even two rides that, sometimes, somehow become one, if you're willing to bend your brain around that. In most cases, we refer to those as *subplots*—the main story is your A-Plot, and subsequent smaller plots are your B-Plot, your C-Plot, and so on and so forth. These plots may or may not be woven in together.

This is fine, and nobody would fault you for looking at narrative this way if you find it helpful.

But I'm going to go a different way.

Worry less about individual subplots, especially as an offshoot of that complicated word *plot*.

Instead, assume (hopefully quite correctly) that your story comprises a number of characters, all of whom have their own problems and desires and, in the pursuit of solutions and answers, create their own stories. Sometimes these stories form the thrust of the larger narrative, sometimes they form smaller journeys—like taking an exit off a main highway for a while to see the sights. These smaller narratives are what you would consider subplots, but don't worry about labeling them. Mostly the goal is to let them again be character originated and character driven. Just because they don't become the main thrust of the story doesn't mean they're not important—especially not to the characters on those journeys, right? We don't need to call them subplots.

Instead, think of them as story threads.

A thread is woven into the tapestry. And further, a thread is best when it's not left hanging—meaning, these "subplots" will eventually tie back into the whole, binding with the narrative overall. They aren't disconnected. They don't hang loose. Take these threads and tie them to other threads—to the fabric as a whole.

You can look at it this way: Every character has one *main* problem and then a series of *smaller* problems—as few as one or as many as you need. (Though again, heed the rule: Don't let more snakes out of the bag than you can kill.) A main character or protagonist can take side deviations that address smaller problems—and you deal with these the same way we discussed in the last chapter. A problem has a solution, and in pursuit of that solution comes the potential for story. In *Lost*, all of the characters had side stories that spawned in part from their backstories—this gave them depth and complexity, and assured that not all of their problems stemmed purely from their present time on the mysterious island. Television shows, comics, and even novels *tend* to have more space than other media, and thus, greater opportunity to explore a character and her problems fully.

The larger problem is the rope; the smaller problems are threads. Buffy's desire to be a normal high school girl while having to fight vampires *and* having a vampire boyfriend—that's the rope of the show. It's the thing we use to grab hold of and pull ourselves through that narrative. But every episode yields new threads: Buffy's relationship to her mother, to her teachers, to Giles the Watcher, and on and on. She has a lot of smaller problems that don't dominate the show overall, but that dominate one episode or one season.

(Some video games offer a nice angle on this, too. A role-playing game like *Skyrim* or *Mass Effect*—or even any game similar to *Metroid*—lets you take your character on a variety of "side quests" or ancillary missions to complete different goals, which might include getting a better weapon or answering a question about your backstory or defeating some ancient, irritable goblin king.)

Also worth noting is that these story threads can interact much as the characters themselves do. So-called subplots can either intersect at a perpendicular angle, meaning they slam into the main story and affect it in a head-on-collision kind of way. Or they run parallel, meaning they may never tie in to the main story so as to actively affect it, but they still grow and change the character in interesting ways that passively affects the main story—or, at least, reflects upon it. And, just as with characters, these individual story threads can be *neither* perpendicular nor parallel, meaning they will eventually intersect, though not at a hard right angle—it will be more like two cars traveling on the highway changing lanes, gently passing and crossing one another. Some effect will occur, but until both cars need to take the same exit off of the highway, it's just trading paint.

Example? Well, in *The Princess Bride*, you know Inigo Montoya's saying, right? You can say it with me now. Say it aloud, here we go:

"HELLO, MY NAME IS INIGO MONTOYA, YOU STOLE MY SCOOBY DOO LUNCHBOX, PREPARE ... FOR SPANKINGS."

is handed a note

I am informed by my pop culture lawyers that this is actually incorrect.

Apologies to all, and especially to William Goldman and Mandy Patinkin. Let's try this again:

"HELLO, MY NAME IS INIGO MONTOYA. YOU KILLED MY FATHER. PREPARE ... TO DIE."

That line is integral to his story and, ultimately, sums up his quest. The background is that his father made a special sword for a very bad man, the six-fingered Count Rugen, and then Rugen killed the father and scarred the son. So Inigo devotes his entire life to mastering the blade in order to exact his revenge. It's not the main thrust of *The Princess Bride* (though I'd maybe argue that Rugen's comeuppance is the most satisfying moment in the whole movie), but as a story thread, it works perfectly. It's neither perpendicular nor parallel—it slowly but surely moves toward the main plot, finally intersecting when he needs to rescue Westley from death to exact his revenge (and, of course, Westley needs Inigo to resurrect him in order to reclaim his love, Buttercup). Those two stories feed one another, clearly weaving together by the end—but the story threads aren't antithetical or antagonistic, either. They dovetail and become one. Inigo's story is essential to the story just the same.

And therein lies another lesson.

The decision to include a story thread—a "subplot"—is really about answering, "Is this essential? Does it add to the narrative? Does it shape the overall story and deepen our experience? Does it help to change or reveal one or several of the characters?" If yes, go for it.

If no ... then maybe you've a darling that demands to be killed.

Interlude

THE FOURTH RULE

It is routinely accepted that the job of your story is first to entertain.

That may be true enough—certainly if the audience is not captivated and held in thrall by the story, they might eject.

But *entertainment* is also a pretty threadbare goal. I'd argue that it's not enough merely to entertain. Also, entertainment as a goal sits right at the bottom of the barrel. We're not jugglers. I'm not your court jester, and you're not mine, either. As Darth Vader said in *Star Wars*: "Am I funny how, I mean funny like I'm a clown, do I amuse you? Do I make you laugh, am I here to fuckin' amuse you?" I'm pretty sure it was Vader who said that. Maybe it was the Emperor[1]. Whatever. Toe-MAY-toe, toe-MAH-toe.

Let's thicken the stew, shall we?

---

[1] Correction: It was Artoo. You just couldn't understand him with all the *bleets* and *bloops*.

The best thing a story can do is, in this order:

1. Make the audience *feel*.
2. Make the audience *think*.
3. *Entertain* the audience.

Now, you could rightly argue that *entertainment* is actually a subset of the first one: You can make them *feel* entertained, and that's true to a point; I just want to keep it separate so we maintain that entertainment is its own independent entity.

So, let's say you go to the movies.

What's the best outcome of seeing that movie? When you walk out of the theater, probably with some friends or a loved one or your family, what's the ideal *result*? It's when you walk out and the first thing you want to do is go somewhere, get a hamburger or a slice of pie, and hunker down and *talk about it*. And the first reason you want to talk about it is that the movie stoked your emotions. It played you like a guitar, plucking your heartstrings, making you sing sad songs, then happy ones, then triumphant ones. It ran you through a gamut of emotions, and you just have to share them. Then—*then!*— you calm down and get to the stuff that the movie gave you to chew on. It gave your brain something to do: Was so-and-so his father? What happened at the end could mean that the story isn't over, that so-and-so isn't dead, that the other guy was the murderer. What was the movie trying to say, was it that we're all doomed, or that love will lead the way, or that cake is better than pie (*what a vicious lie!*)?

The movie made you feel.

And then it made you think.

And now you wanna go talk about it with a mouth that you have wisely stuffed with pie.

The worst-case scenario is that the movie just sucked. Didn't pluck your strings, didn't give your brain anything to do, didn't even entertain you.

The middle ground is that the movie entertained you.

And only that.

You sit there in the car after, and you and your film-going compatriot (a loved one, a child, a stray dog, a down-on-his-luck koala bear, a mop handle with a bucket on top of it) both casually shrug and half smile and say, "That was good." But what you mean is, "That was *fine*," as in the way you might describe a day where nothing went exactly wrong and nothing went exactly right. It's a piece of white bread. It works for its purpose and tastes *fine* at the time, but leaves no lasting impression.

Entertainment and entertainment *only* is exactly that—

It leaves no impression beyond the moment in which it entertains you.

It was funny. It was exciting. It was good.

It was *fine*.

But the best stories are the ones that hit you in your heart and in your head. The ones that make you feel, and the ones that also make you think.

So let *those* be your goals first. Let entertainment follow.

Chapter Four

FIGHTIN', FORNICATIN', AND FLAPPIN' THEM GUMS: ON CHARACTER INTERACTIONS

At its most basic and bare bones, a story is this:

Characters do shit.

Characters say shit.

Repeat until end.

And even in that, there maybe exists a needless deviation—we often separate *action* and *dialogue* but, really, dialogue *is* action. *Talk* is a verb. To communicate is to do something, perhaps one of the most vital forms of "doing something" that we have available to us as humans.

We often dismiss that, though, right? *Oh, that's just talk.* We pretend like words are not meaningful, like they're just hot air. But that's not true at all. Dialogue and communication are as vital as any other action, and in fact contain layers—because dialogue can be savvier, more sinister, more affecting. Dialogue can convince us to take further action (think Iago manipulating Othello), it can be a lie (think Obi-Wan telling Luke untruths about his father), it can say things without ever saying things (the subtext of class warfare is present in a lot of *Die Hard*'s dialogue).

Dialogue also has value in that it's not just a single character acting alone; it involves characters communicating with each other. And damn, do we love dialogue! Dialogue is story lubricant. It's a fast slide, not a creaky staircase. You ever watch an interview with a compelling subject? It's just two people sitting in conversation, one asking questions, another answering.

Watch a Quentin Tarantino movie and marvel at how much of the story is told through dialogue. Kevin Smith, too, and David Mamet. Smith's first film, *Clerks*, is told almost entirely through dialogue, and with very little actual action. Same with Mamet's *Glengarry Glen Ross*, which began life as a play and later became a film.

A great deal of tension can be earned through simply letting characters *talk*.

Carry it further, and you start to see how every interaction between two characters—fighting, flirting, arguing, screwing each other's brains out—works in similar ways. They follow a certain weave and weft, they work with a certain flow. A fight scene and a love scene are a kind of conversation—and they follow similar rules. (Again, we must remember: The push and pull of question and answer will draw us eagerly through damn near any narrative.)

Let's unpack this a little bit.

CHARACTER THUNDERDOME

You have two characters. Or three. Or five. Maybe it's two lovers squaring off to bang each other on the couch or yell at each other in the kitchen. Maybe it's two boxers in the ring, or three sisters talking about plans to bury their recently deceased father. Could be it's a trial, or a rally, or a galactic star chamber discussing the fate of the known universe.

We begin with some base-level assumptions, which build on the rules we set for Anatomy of a Scene on page 93 of this book.

1. **EVERYBODY WANTS SOMETHING.** This is true in life, and it is triply true inside your story. Characters come together, and they each have a perspective, a problem, and/or a desire. The interaction between the characters, whether it's physical or vocal, or both, factors in this reality: that every character wants something. Which is to say—

2. **CHARACTERS INTERACT WITH PURPOSE.** I treat most interactions between characters as a kind of power exchange … which is not to say that every character wants to dominate every other character, but simply that, in every interaction, a character's purpose is on display. They want something, that something forms their motives, and the interaction is an expression, conscious or unconscious, of them trying to get it. It might be simply that a character wants comfort. He might want love or pleasure. Maybe he wants money, or revenge, or ego stroking. Maybe the characters want the same thing (parallel!) or are at odds (perpendicular). Maybe their motives are known to one another, maybe not. Assume that interactions are loaded for bear with purpose.

3. **INTERACTIONS CONVEY INFORMATION TO THE AUDIENCE *AND* TO THE CHARACTERS.** We should come away from every scene between two characters having learned something. Maybe something small. Could be related to the characters and their prob-

lems or to the "larger story" of the plot. It might answer a question or introduce us to deeper mystery. But at no point should we, the audience, come away without learning something. Further, the *characters* should be able to learn something, too. Maybe it's the wrong information, or maybe it's an assumption, but the characters should leave the exchange with new information, even if the other doesn't know precisely what that entails. Every scene of interaction is an opportunity to convey information—and more than an opportunity, I'd argue it's a necessity. Use your narrative real estate!

4. **INTERACTION LEAVES EACH CHARACTER CHANGED.** Every interaction is an opportunity for a status change. This never needs to be as dramatic as the shift in status quo you get marking the change at each act break, but we want the sense that every character is *affected* by the interaction. The worst shape of a story is a straight line because the straight line is a flat line, and a flat line means *dead*. You don't want the characters to engage each other and come away unscathed, unchanged, precisely and perfectly the same. Two characters don't bed each other and come out status quo. Two characters don't argue or flirt without *something* happening in each of them. What changes can be how they feel about one another or, as above, the information they learn, or a physical injury that occurred as a result (groin pull?). It can be as dramatic as OMG FRIENDSHIP IS OVER or as subtle as *you know, I don't know that I trust you like I used to*. It can be as extreme as "YOU KILLED MY FATHER, PREPARE TO DIE," and as simple as the emotional reward from "That'll do, pig," in *Babe*.

5. **EMPATHY IS EVERYTHING.** In defining my terms, I'm going to strain the dictionary definitions to fit my point a bit, but let's assume that sympathy is about feeling bad for someone, and empathy is about understanding them. Empathy isn't about agreeing—okay? It's just about putting on someone else's shoes and walking a mile in them, and then understanding why they're

Damn Fine Story

mad at us for stealing their shoes. Your job as a storyteller is to have empathy for your characters. It is literally your job to understand them. Further, in a scene of interaction, it's also your job to instill the audience with empathy for the characters. The interaction is there (in part) to help us understand them. Every interaction builds a bridge toward them and brings the audience closer to them.

That doesn't mean it's designed to deliver *sympathy*. We don't need to feel for them. We just need to get it. We need to get where they're coming from, even if we hate it, hate them, hate everything they stand for. Empathy is about context, and an interaction helps provide that contextual understanding.

6. **EVERY INTERACTION HAS TWO LAYERS.** The first layer is the visible, textual layer. It's the fight, the trial, the argument. She says this, he says that, she does this in response, he reacts accordingly, and on and on. But a second layer lurks underneath: The exchange *means* something. There exists a subtextual component. A lot waits unspoken. Theme lurks in the wings. So much of an interaction isn't about what they're saying or doing—it's about what they're *not* saying or doing. It's why they're there at all. Look at it this way: When you ask a significant other how they're doing and they respond tersely with, "I'm *fine*," then you can be pretty damn sure that they are the farthest thing from fine. The first layer is what they said, but the subtextual layer tells us so much more. Even if they never crack open and spill what's really bothering them, we still know—*something is there.*

7. **EVERY INTERACTION MUST BRING TENSION.** Conversation is conflict. When we say tension, it needn't be *edge-of-your-seat, oh god I've just bitten my fingernails down to bloody nubs* kind of tension. It doesn't mean you clench your sphincter so tightly it could bend rebar. It just means we don't know what's going to happen. Characters interacting are engaging in an invisible act of tug-of-war. They're pushing and pulling on one another. Sometimes

the rope has slack; other times it's taut as a strangler's cord. But either way, the gulf between characters is one that carries and conveys tension. An interaction is a negotiation of sorts, and negotiations bring tension. And part of that tension comes from the fact that interactions bring mystery: As noted, we don't know the outcome of an interaction until it happens, and so, throughout, we have questions.

TIPS ON WRITING GREAT DIALOGUE

Writing dialogue is easy in the same way that painting a picture is easy: Anybody can just slap paint on a canvas and say, "LOOK AT THESE PRETTY LITTLE TREES," but that doesn't make them Bob Ross. And anybody can smash dialogue into character's mouths, but not everybody is Elmore Leonard or Toni Morrison, right?

Let's talk some tips that will help you refine your dialogue:

- **JUST LET THEM TALK.** Put two or four, or however many characters you need, right there on the page, and let them talk. Let them talk for as long and as much as you want. Don't worry about how many words or script pages it takes up. They can have an *epic* conversation, and you are free to let it ricochet from topic to topic, whether it's the problem at hand or a bad back or a cheating lover, anything and everything. But here's the trick: *That's not where you stop.* This is just a first draft, and you will need to pare the conversation down, down, down, until the shaggy beast is now a prim poodle. Look at it this way: It's like digital photography. The great joy of digital photography for me is that I can take one hundred shots just to get one good image. Eighty of them will be garbage, nineteen will be questionable at best, and one—one!—will be worth keeping and displaying. I'm not suggesting that you will only keep one percent of the dialogue that you write, but I *am* saying that you should feel free to let the characters ramble, comfortable in the knowledge that you can trim, slice, and chop when it comes time to redraft the second, third, or forty-fifth iteration.

- **ITS SHAPE DETERMINES ITS PACE.** Think of the quick-witted, quick-tongued, and sharp-as-a-dagger dialogue of Shakespeare—or its modern variant, *Gilmore Girls*.[1] Watch Shakespeare (or, again, *Gilmore Girls*) and note how the dialogue moves as quick as the snapping of one's fingers, each line spoken with the whip-slash panache of a fencer's épée. Then watch Oliver Stone's *JFK*, and notice how the dialogue is heavier, weightier, more ponderous. This is true of almost any historical drama, actually—and that slowness of language slows the narrative, giving it the depth and density one expects history to possess. A single story can have both styles of dialogue, too: In *Die Hard*, a lot of the characters snap back and forth, like in the Hans and John dialogue noted on page 63 of this very book. But then you look at the scenes where McClane and Al Powell talk about themselves, and their dialogue taps the brakes and eases the thrilling pace of the story. It needs to do that to deliver oxygen into the narrative—and, most vitally, to make us care about these two characters. Short, quippy bits wouldn't give us enough. People don't spill their guts to each other in short quips.

- **TELLING *IS* SHOWING.** It is one of those supposedly ironclad rules that storytellers should not *tell* us things—rather, they must *show* us things. And that's true to a point. If you're writing a novel, you don't need to say, "Bob was angry," because you can show him being angry—clenching his fists, his forehead veins throbbing, kicking his chair, whatever. And in a script, you might *say* Bob is angry, but the actor will demonstrate that onscreen (and in a comic, the artist would depict the emotion visually). And yet, dialogue is a huge part of storytelling—and in dialogue, characters

---

[1] Search your heart, you know it to be true.

tell each other things. The trick here, then, is to never have characters speak—instead, they convey information through hand gestures and interpretive dance and—*receives a note* okay that might not be right? Let me consult this other stack of notes here, hold on, hold on … ah! The *real* trick here is to avoid making a character's dialogue clunky and expository. We don't want them to needlessly explain (or rather, *over*explain) things. The way a character talks—what words she uses, her cadence, her openness, or her reticence—speaks to more than just the words coming out of her imaginary mouth.

• **AVOID ON-THE-NOSE DIALOGUE.** Characters are not explanation machines, nor are they dispensaries of factual reality. They should constantly spill their genuine feelings or their plans. They should *not* exposit boldly or dully about what is actually going on around them. On-the-nose dialogue lacks subtlety and nuance, and is often totally needless. Often what's most interesting about a character is what she doesn't *want* to say. It's all about what characters are keeping in, not what they're letting out. Dialogue is at its *most* interesting when it acts as a power play between the characters, each trying to get the other to open up while simultaneously working to keep their own secrets or fears buried. What they *don't* say is often as interesting as what they *do*.

• **SEEK AUTHENTICITY OVER REALITY.** Some writers try very hard to capture dialogue exactly as it sounds between two real people, with all its local color, all its fits and starts, all its interruptions. Don't do this. It almost never works unless it's in the hands of a master storyteller. In dialogue, and really in all storytelling, you want to avoid reality because reality is bad. Reality is cheap and crass and often too dull or too weird to serve as fiction and, in reality, dialogue often sounds clunky and awkward because … honestly, that's how people communicate. In fiction, you are afforded no such luxury, nor do you really want that. Instead, aim for authenticity. You want it to *feel* real. You want to ape a few patterns, and use a few choice contractions or tidbits of local color. You don't want every *uhhh umm well ahhh nnngh* in there, but one or two, here and there, are fine. You want it to *feel* like it's real dialogue without it actually *being* real dialogue. In fact, look at this dialogue from Joel and Ethan Coen's *Fargo*:

> **JERRY:** I'm, uh, Jerry Lundegaard—
> **CARL:** You're Jerry Lundegaard?
> **JERRY:** Yah, Shep Proudfoot said—
> **CARL:** Shep said you'd be here at 7:30. What gives, man?
> **JERRY:** Shep said 8:30.
> **CARL:** We been sitting here an hour. I've peed three times already.
> **JERRY:** I'm sure sorry. I—Shep told me 8:30. It was a mix-up, I guess.

- **CHARACTERS DON'T WAIT TO SPEAK.** Dialogue is a back and forth, but it needn't be one that's neat and tidy. People in real life—and so, also in fiction—do not neatly wait for one person to stop talking to properly and politely respond. They talk over one another and interrupt each other (as evidenced above in the *Fargo* bit). Further, how often they do that speaks to who the character is. In the Carl and Jerry scene above, you can see Jerry being hesitant and polite, whereas Carl is irritated, maybe even aggressive.
- **CONSIDER THE RHYTHM OF DIALOGUE.** Rhythm is an important part of writing and storytelling overall, as noted on page 102. You want a sense of movement in a scene of dialogue—characters squaring off, feeling out each other's positions, testing waters. Tension increases, and a revelation mounts—until suddenly one of them switches gears and changes the subject just as we get close to the truth. (Once more, the metaphor of the roller coaster is apt.) The shape of dialogue matters, too, and not just in determining pace—but our eye and our ear strive for variation. On a novel page, we want to see short spikes of text breaking into a longer paragraph. We want a handful of short sentences and

declarations broken up with a longer confession or confrontation. You want the dialogue you read in your head—or, ideally, out loud—to sound the way it's supposed to sound onscreen. It should ring true, or at least authentic, and rhythm goes a long way to making that happen. (I advocate reading your work aloud because you *hear* things that your eyes will miss.) You want to mix it up. Keep it variable. That variability—that rhythm—keeps the audience on edge. You want them always on their toes, unsure of where the dialogue is going, or where it will take them. Two quick exercises to follow rhythm in dialogue: First, listen to people having a conversation in public, and write it down. Second, write down the dialogue in a scene of a film or on television—don't copy the script, write down the dialogue as they say it. You'll see the ebb-and-flow of conversation. You'll spy the rhythm at work.

- **DIALOGUE IS DNA.** Every character is different … and here's where you say, "Hey thanks, Captain Obvious, next you're going to tell us that WATER IS WET or that OTTERS ARE ADORABLE."[2] What is important to realize, however, is not merely that characters are different, but how those differences are best expressed—and dialogue is one of the chief-most ways to do that.

Characters distinguish themselves by their choices, and dialogue informs, explains, and bolsters those choices. What it really means for you as the storyteller is that dialogue needs to feel like it belongs to the person who's saying it. It shouldn't sound just like you. It shouldn't sound like every other character. Some of this is surface impression: cadence, word choice, slang terms used. Some of this is deeper: the character's passions, the character's *choices*, what she chooses to talk about ver-

---

[2] Otters really *are* adorable. I'm sure I'm misusing the footnote format to emphasize that, but c'mon. Let's all just take a minute, lean back, close our eyes, and imagine otters. There. Yeah. Otters. … Boom, your entire day just improved by a factor of "otters."

sus what she chooses to hide. One character is terse with a military precision to her language—especially when she discusses the military, since she's a soldier. Another character is loose and rambly, and he goes on at length about conspiracy theories and other paranoid nonsense. One character curses. Another is unfailingly positive. You want all of them to feel like themselves when they speak.

No better test for this exists than simply writing down the dialogue and cutting out any kind of dialogue attribution, whether on the novel page or in a script. Write the dialogue without identifying who is saying what, and test yourself—and any beta readers or editors you have—with the task of figuring out who is saying what. If it's difficult to determine, then you might need to do a better job making each line of dialogue like a fingerprint of the character that's saying it.

Once again, look at that Carl and Jerry dialogue from *Fargo* above. Or the McClane and Gruber dialogue on page 63. Even if you hadn't seen each film, each character's dialogue stands out and feels unique.

- **ACTION, ACTION, ACTION.** Give them something to do while talking. Maybe they're running. Maybe one person is messing up the kitchen while the other is tidying up behind them. Maybe they're all gathered around, getting drunk, grooming otters, or trying to disarm a nuclear bomb. The trick is to match the tenor and content of the dialogue with the action—postcoital bliss might be a good time for long ruminations, but not when you're disarming a bomb. However, while disarming a bomb, characters might be more truthful or confessional. The action and the words need to make sense together. It needs to feel organic and connected to the situation.

WRITING FIGHTING IS LIKE WRITING FUCKING

Writing sex is like writing a fight scene.

Consider:

Sex and violence stare at one another in a warped carnival mirror. Both are intimate. Both reflect physicality. Heartbeats pulse. Fluids spurt—spit, blood, sweat.

Form and function do well together across all types of writing, but this is *particularly* true in terms of writing both action *and* sex. I find that when I write these, the *form* of my writing moves to match the pacing of the action.[3] Something that's meant to be fast and brutal—a short, sharp shock such as two pugilists pounding away at one another or two sexual partners in a one-night stand, erm, pounding away at each other might demand shorter sentences, or sentence fragments, or blunt and forward language.

Alternately, you may want to slow things down—stretching the narrative scene out with more languid pacing and language. To give the sense of a fight scene being slower and more strategic—or a sex scene being dreamlike or strange, the participants taking their time with each other.

There also exists the consideration of sensation: Both fighting and sex scenes aren't just about the, ahem, mechanical blow-by-blow, but also about what the characters are experiencing in terms of feelings, both physical and emotional. The scene needn't be described like a karate manual or a health class video on sexual intercourse. Some mix must be in play. I've read scenes that clarify every tiny detail—the story telegraphs every thrown punch, every grenade tossed, every penetrative moment, every bite, kiss, or scratch. This is nice in a lot of ways. Necessary, even, if only because it helps you maintain an image in the audience's head of what's going on.

---

[3] Or, "action." Get it? Wink-wink? Nudge-nudge? "Action" *eyebrow waggle*.

On the *other* hand, that can get a little dull. A giant meaty paragraph dictating the cold and clinical step by step of a fight or sex scene is a paragraph I am going to ice skate over with my eyes. This is doubly true of those writers who know martial arts and write about it in a very granular way. No, I don't know what a Wily Cheung Dragon Five-Toed Pylon Garrote-Kick does, and I don't really care. Nor do I need to know what comprises various sex moves.[4] Further, and perhaps more importantly, these fighting and sex scenes needn't only be action scenes.

Any such scene is awesome when it's doing *more* than just expressing physical action (pain! pleasure! pizazz!) and a sequence of objective events. How can you reveal character in a scene of fighting or sex? How can you express theme and mood? During a scene of romance or battle, a character is ultimately *exposed*. A blustery character becomes suddenly timid. An uncertain character becomes bold and brave in the moment. A character reveals traits of being a caretaker—or a sadist. Themes emerge: competition between characters, lovemaking saving the day, the complicated nature of human interaction.

Just as dialogue and description are given over to subtext, sexytimes and punchy-punchy-times can be given over to subtler threads, too. Such a scene should never be there just because it's obligatory: It should always have deeper purpose. Even if that purpose is just to reveal the interplay and power-exchanges between characters—and trust me, just as a scene of two people fighting is about an exchange of power, so is a scene of sex and love. Who is on top (literally and figuratively)? Who stands to gain from this? What will the consequences be when this scene of love or war concludes?

A scene of sex or fighting doesn't stop a character from being who that character is. It *reveals* it. Selfish. Selfless. Nervous. Anxious. Afraid. Angry. Griefstricken. How characters fight or, erm, "do

---

[4] Like the "Arizona Tugboat," the "Schenectady Trampoline," or the altogether more rare and ancient "Monkey Steals The Possum Toes."

the sex" says a helluva lot about them. They're not automatons. Such physical confrontations can be raw, abrasive, illustrative. They tear away our barriers, our armor. So show that as part of the story. Let it expose them. Let the plot change as a result of the scene of punching, kicking, shooting, kissing, groping, screwing.

There's value in seeing the relationship between *fighting* and *fucking*, at least in terms of writing. Bring one into the other. Bring the intimacy and discomfort of sex into the fight scenes, and bring our culture's comfort with violence into writing the bedroom scenes. An interesting exercise: Write a sex scene like you're writing a fight scene.

Speaking of exercises …

EXERCISES FOR CHARACTER INTERACTIONS

One option to help you get a grip on *character interactions* in your story is to perform some exercises—no, not jumping jacks, not hot yoga, not pickleball[5]—that are focused on helping you understand the characters you're writing and how they intersect. Use or discard at your leisure.

The Character Logline, Which Has Nothing to Do with Logs

A logline is this: It's a single sentence meant to *very loosely* describe your book or your movie or whatever it is you're writing (comic book, manifesto, diner menu). This is similar in a sense to an elevator pitch—a quick, 10-second hot-take on the story at hand. It's not meant to give an entire scope of the book, but it's meant to *entice* and *excite*. "A take-no-shit cop from New York travels to California to mend his broken marriage but must contend with terrorists who

---

[5] A waste of perfectly good pickles, if you ask me.

have taken his wife hostage in her office building." Obviously, that is a logline I just made up for ~~The Princess Bride~~ I mean *Die Hard*. Generally, loglines are *story*-driven. You get one per story. Easy. Except I like to sometimes think of loglines too for each of my characters. Just to help me crystallize who they are, so when it comes time to have those characters interact with each other, I know their stories, I know their problems, I know what brings them to the page and what they want from each other.

So, a logline for John McClane might be: "Stubborn, impulsive New York City cop who will do anything to save his marriage—and save the day."

A logline for Hans Gruber: "Smug Eurotrash thief who is a master strategist and who cloaks the theft of $640 million in bearer bonds as an act of political terror."

Sergeant Al Powell: "Sad-sack, desk-bound LAPD cop who remains haunted to inaction by the last time he pulled the trigger and killed an innocent kid carrying a toy gun."

Even if there were zero other characters in the movie, already I can start to envision how these characters might play off each other. (And to go back to our directional relationships, it's easy to see how these characters might run perpendicular or parallel to one another.)

Post-It Notes as Far as the Eye Can See

If you want something less codified but more granular, I like to sometimes take a single Post-it note per character and write down on it a series of traits. What you write there varies by character, but I like to sometimes include:

- Three adjectives that describe him.
- His overarching problem and proposed solution.
- Any limitations that internally complicate him.
- And, if possible, an expected three-beat arc to drive home how I anticipate he'll change over the course of the story.

Then I stick them all around me as I write—on the monitor, on my desk, to my elbows and knees, to the outside of my eyeglasses facing in. Okay, maybe I don't get *that* extreme, but you get the point.

Then, as I write, I update them. Particularly, as characters interact, I may write more on that note—or add further notes—that indicate how characters are relating to one another. Which leads me to:

The Relationship Web

On a piece of paper, write down each character's name in a circle. Then draw arrows from each character to each other character. Connect them with lines, and along those lines write a single descriptive statement indicating that character's feelings toward the other character (the one the arrow points to).

So, Steve → is in love with → Becky.
But, Becky → believes Steve to be a stalker → Steve.

As other characters are added in, the web grows more complex:

Jeremy → worships his brother Steve → Steve.
Steve → uses and abuses his little brother → Jeremy.

Jeremy → has a soft spot for → Becky.
Becky → wants to save Jeremy and get him away from Steve's influence → Steve.

And onward. The greater the web grows, the more of the push-and-pull you see amidst the weave-and-weft of connecting strands.

The Character Test-Drive, Vroom Vroom

This is a thing that I do, and it is a thing *you* may want to do, as well.

When we begin to write a story, it's like meeting a new group of friends in an unfamiliar place. It's you driving to a mall in a part of town you've never seen, then hanging out with a pack of strangers who you are now committed to remain with for a period of time. It's weird and uncomfortable. And in a story, of course, you have to hit the ground running. You can't dally. You gotta move, move, *move*.

What I do before I actually start the story is this:

I take the characters on a test drive. I open up a Word document, and I pick up the characters I want to write about, and I drop them into the wide-open white space of the page as if they are action figures on my living room floor. I give them a problem. I force them to interact. And then I write. I write for as long as I want to. But I do *not* write them into the story, and I do not focus on the tale I want to inevitably tell with them. Instead, I let them talk. I let them act. I let them interact. No limits. No rules. And no expectation that I will ever keep what I've written.

The value of this for me is that it establishes a baseline. I become familiar with the characters. I see tics and habits emerge. And, despite knowing full well that what I wrote should be garbage, I usually end up finding things in there I *do* want to keep—a funny joke, an unanticipated trait, an emergent behavior. Try it out. Report back. I'll wait here. Trapped in this book because of an old wizard's curse!

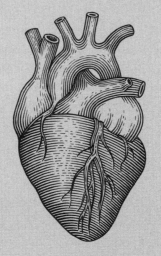

Interlude

THE FIFTH RULE

When it comes to writing advice, we are fond of slavishly roasting a number of old chestnuts again and again—we recycle and recirculate these tired old "unswerving laws of telling stories" as if they are gospel truth and to deny them is to deny the godliness of what we do.

We tell people: Writers write, storywriters don't use adverbs, novelists always use the dialogue tag *said*. We say to open with a bang, we demand they don't open with weather or a character looking at herself in the mirror (oops, I've done both), don't have an unlikable protagonist (also oops), don't use a thesaurus, don't write a prologue, and so on.

One of the most famous, and most debated, is this:

Write what you know.

And of course, nobody knows what the hell that means. How would they? It's a four-word proclamation—and, generally, short proclamations are a very good way to grind nuance down underneath a twisting boot heel. Does it mean that what goes onto the page is only information that I know? If I want to write about flying a dragon, does that mean I can't because I've never actually flown a dragon? Or does it mean I should try to find some *common experience*, some aspect of my life that I can use to relate to what's happening on the page? Does it mean I should never write characters who are unlike me? Should all my stories just be stories of dumb white dudes in semirural Pennsyltucky, dudes who sit in sheds and write books? Is this why Stephen King so often writes protagonists who are writers?

Is the saying "write what you know" a prohibition against straying into unfamiliar, unrelatable, and ultimately unreliable territory? Or is it an opportunity for the author to know more? Is it a locked door, or the key to open a locked door? Is it an invitation to authenticity, or a proclamation demanding you stay in your lane?

I have no idea. I don't even know who said it, originally, as it has been attributed to both Twain and Hemingway. What I do know is that it is either a piece of very good advice written poorly, or a piece of poor advice written elegantly. I know that a strict reading of it is nonsense. Any interpretation must favor the loosier-goosier approach of assuming that it is not a prohibition against going outside your authorial comfort zone but, instead, a call to look at your own experiences and find some way to use them—and when your own experiences don't meet muster, to go have new experiences. Or, hell with it, just fake it.

I suspect the advice is better when you expect it means to say, "Write what you understand," with the unspoken addendum of, "If you don't know what you're writing about, go learn more stuff, you clod." Those four words add up to an incomplete piece of writing advice that has plagued us.

I say scrap 'em.

And in the pantheon of MIGHTY STORYTELLING LAWS, replace it with this, which is certainly no longer and arguably no less open to interpretation, but hopefully it gets us to a better place:

Write who you are.

What that means is this: What you know isn't much of a watermark for what you should or shouldn't write. We know a lot of true things, we know a lot of false things, we have heads full of data both real and imagined. We can always go "know" more stuff because we are creatures who can read books and talk to other humans and have experiences. We're covered on that front.

Who we are is what matters most. And that's because who we are is largely indefatigable—we can't really help it. We are a bundle of thoughts and feelings born of both nature and nurture. We are a complex tangle of inaccuracies, inconsistencies, and ideas. We are bloated with certainties and haunted by uncertainties. We each have genetic code, but in a sense we have a memetic code,[1] too: an uncharted map, an emotional genome, that informs us and *completes* us, even as we feel woefully incomplete.

That's what goes into your story.

Your story is more than who you are, but at its core it's still you. We are often wont to note how there are so few original stories, and that's true—moreover, that's totally fine. Because when telling any story, the one original thing that comes to the table is *you*. You are a unique arrangement. We are at our best as storytellers when who we are—the ideas we hold, the loved ones we've known, the places we've lived, the fears we have—helps to inform the stories we write. That's how we put ourselves out there. Not by relying on data or in-

---

[1] The origin of the word "meme," by the way.

formation, not by worrying about what's in our heads but, rather, about what's in our hearts.

Write who you are. Crack open your breastbone, grab your heart from its visceral mooring, and smash it into the page. Give it a few bloody twists just to make sure your heart print is firmly and forever smashed onto the page.

Your stories are you, and you are your stories.

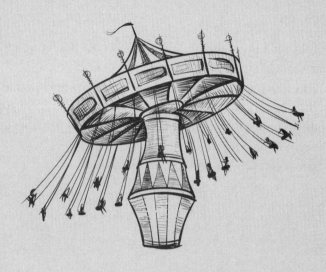

Chapter Five

WHAT HIDES BEHIND THE WALLS: UNDERSTANDING A STORY'S THEME

I had an eighth-grade teacher, and this teacher, in the span of a single year, made me

1. decide to never be a writer,
   and then
2. decide like hell I was damn sure gonna be a writer just to spite her.

That spite was an important component in me wanting to be a writer, and it came from my observance—as a stupid eighth-grade student—that I knew things she clearly did not know. Because she was wrong about stuff. Provably wrong. And I don't mean like, I was young, and I thought I knew better. I've been there, too, and more often than not, but I've learned (as one should) that most of the time when I thought I was being smart, I was really just being a smart-*ass*. But this isn't that.

This is like a math teacher telling you $4 + 4 = 9$.

Here's what it was:

I would write papers or stories, and I would use words that she would routinely tell me were not real words. "You made that word up," she would say to me, yet again disappointed that I was apparently inventing a brand-new vocabulary for my work. Except I wasn't. These were real words. And whenever she'd tell me this, I'd have to go and pull out the book where I found the word in the first place— sometimes in a story by an author *we were reading for class*—and point to it, petulant and angry. "Here is the word. It exists." And she'd reluctantly adjust my grade, raising it slightly. I remember a particularly egregious example where I used the word *rictus*. I don't know if I knew *precisely* what the word even meant, honestly, but I'd seen it in like, half a dozen horror novels, and so when I used it, she called me on it and again uttered that familiar refrain: "This isn't a real word." So I hauled out the book I was reading—pretty sure it was a Robert McCammon novel, maybe *Swan Song*—and with my index finger stabbed the middle of the page where the word lived, *poke poke poke*.

Then she had the gall to say: "That writer just made that word up."

Which felt like a smack in the face. To me, what had been written was canonical. If you were an author and you wrote a book, what you did was holy writ. It was chiseled into the fundamental bedrock of language. You had earned your place and could not be laid low by the dismissive hand of my eighth-grade English teacher, goddamnit.

But then I was like, *Oh no, maybe that author did make the word up.*

This was in the days before we all had All the World's Information tightly packed into an electronic talking brick in our pockets, so I couldn't just whip out my iPhone and Google the word and wave it around triumphantly. This was like four hundred years ago, when you had to move the sack of flesh called a "human body" toward a book called a "dictionary," and I had to haul out said dictionary and point to the evidence. Except our classroom dictionary was basically garbage. It was one of those smaller dictionaries, catechism size, the ones that cannot possibly contain the overgrown breadth and depth of the English language.

It did *not*, in fact, contain the word *rictus*.

Smug and having won this battle, she insisted that the red mark stay on my paper. A minus. A ding in the paint.

Grr.

I was haunted by this. Haunted first by the fear that writers were full of shit, just making up words willy-nilly,[1] and second by the fear that there was no one to trust and that my teacher was somehow right (gasp). But I still felt a spark of hope. I had to believe that my favorite writer would not have led me astray with some nonsense word. It had to be real!

So, the next day, I escalated the fight, and I went down to the ancient temple of knowledge called a "library," and there I found the big-ass, mamma-jamma dictionary. You know the one. You've seen it. It's big enough to bludgeon a stampeding wildebeest. It's got words in there that have not been uttered by a human mouth in three centuries. It's dusty and massive, and has the weight of a book written by the gods themselves.

I flipped through it, page by arduous page, until I found it:

Rictus (n): a fixed grimace or grin.

Ha ha ha! Victory! Triumph! And I'd even used it correctly to describe the face of a desiccated corpse. (It's a good bet that if I went

[1] Like, say, "willy-nilly."

through the public education system today I would've had mandated therapy, since I wrote an endless array of creepy horror stories.) I do not precisely recall *how* I was able to deliver the news to my teacher—again, I did not have a camera phone, and if I tried to put that book on a copy machine, I feared the copy machine would collapse like a house of cards. I expect I probably lashed the dictionary to the ass-end of a cantankerous mule and hauled it to the classroom, where I was able to declare my superiority and get that red mark removed.

Some teachers—many of them in fact—will foster a love of learning in you. Others will make you hate the subject you're studying, sometimes to the point of angrily finding a way to reclaim that subject for yourself.

This teacher was clearly one of the latter.

She did a very good job of making reading and writing and studying literature an act of misery. Everything had a hard-and-fast answer, and even great, wonderful stories—stories by Hawthorne, by Du Maurier, by Shirley Jackson—were deflated with the teacher's pin. She dissected them not as you would a work of art, but more as you would an equation or an earthworm. HERE IS THE STORY'S ALIMENTARY CANAL, WHERE SHIRLEY JACKSON EXCRETES WORD SLURRY THROUGH THE NARRATIVE ANUS.[2] We students read these stories and wanted to talk about how they made us feel, what they made us think, why the author wrote them—and she just wanted to dissect each story the same way, the same time, demanding hard-and-fast answers the same way you might demand of a student the dates of royal succession in England or a list of the American presidents in order. It was rote. It was dull.

And one of the worst examples of this, one that did its damage for *years to come*, was the section she taught on *theme*.

Even now, I can't repress a little shudder.

I confess, I fail to remember the exact details of what was taught, though I remember the basics. I remember her droning on, say-

---

[2] THE NARRATIVE ANUS is my next writing book. Pre-order now!

ing, "There are five universal themes," and then listing them like a menu of options at an oil change place: "Man versus Man. Man versus Self. Man versus Society. Man versus Nature. Man versus Home Appliances."

(I might be misremembering that last one.)

Every story we read, we had to apply one of these five literary themes—never mind the fact they're more like "core conflicts" rather than "themes," but pssh, whatever. With some stories, it's easy enough, right? With Du Maurier's "The Birds," you'd say, okay, it's man versus nature. With Jackson's "The Lottery," it's man versus society. Right? Except on that second one, I remember hands going up and kids asking questions like, "But isn't it also sorta kinda man versus man? Isn't it man versus *human* nature? Given that the person stoned at the end of the story is a woman, why does it have to be *man* versus anything? Can't it be woman versus man? Or woman versus society?"

All those questions were treated almost as if they were a kind of dissent, like we were somehow choosing to interpret a black sky as a blue sky, like we called a cat a dog and said up was down and, sure, we *can* chew bubble gum with our butts. Questions like these were not answered with, "Well, that's an interesting idea, let's explore it," but simply with a rubber stamp that boldly, grumpily declared: WRONG.

We were told that authors had concrete intentions, and stories and poems contained hard-and-fast answers about all things.

Full stop, game over, moving on.

Except.

Except.

Let's hear what Shirley Jackson *actually* had to say about the story.

She said, in an interview in a July issue of the *San Francisco Chronicle* (emphasis mine): "**Explaining just what I had hoped the story to say is very difficult.** I suppose, I hoped, by setting a particularly brutal ancient rite in the present and in my own village, to shock the story's readers with a graphic dramatization of the pointless violence and general inhumanity in their own lives."

To paraphrase, she did not know exactly what the story was trying to say, and she knows it has something to do with ritual, violence, and inhumanity. Which is to say, man versus society still works, but perhaps so does man versus man. Or man versus government, or man versus tradition, or man versus his own worst terrible instincts—all of which, I suppose, you could slot in one of those five conflict themes, but to do so would be an act without nuance. It's like looking at the sky at sunset and instead of describing strata of fluffy pinks and smeary lavenders, just saying bluntly, "IT'S PURPLE. IT'S ALL PURPLE. WHEN THE SKY GOD MADE THE SKY, THE SKY GOD INTENDED ONE COLOR TO BE SEEN, AND THAT COLOR IS PURPLE. DO NOT DENY THIS TRUTH, OR WE WILL SURROUND YOU AND THROW STONES AT YOUR HEAD UNTIL YOU DIE, HERETIC."

Looking for hard and fast answers when reading stories—or when writing them!—is a very good way to diminish what's powerful about stories. They are multifarious, multifaceted things. A story is not a thing given over to concrete rules. As I am wont to say again and again: *This shit ain't math.* A story is not the culmination of a string of numbers. Yes, there are mathlike metaphors to be had when writing a story—how the components of the tale find balance, how we discuss parallel or perpendicular elements, how different plot points add up to certain consequential outcomes. But just the same, you can't take a story and rip it apart and identify its data, its major organs, its perfectly created mathematical components. Stories are far surlier, far more *slippery*, than that. And it's evident right there in Jackson's own words.

She did not know exactly what she was aiming to say.

Jackson had ideas, yes. She had a *hope* as to what she was conveying. Certainly she came to the story with some sense of what would get packed in there, yes, but that doesn't equate to there being a single answer.

What's this mean for you, and for this book?

It means that when you write a story, your story is a product of you. You have all this *stuff* inside your head—ideas, opinions, questions, fears—swirling around in a vital brain maelstrom, and your story is often where you disgorge this mental detritus. It means that your story has all this emotional and intellectual material baked into it, whether you mean it to or not. It means that just as it is your job as an author to make the audience *feel* and *think*, there also exists a pretty good chance that your story is something that makes *you* feel and think, too—after all, it's a product of your thoughts and feelings. If your story is architecture, then these thoughts and feelings are what hide behind the drywall. They lurk between the studs, they crawl through the vents, they hiss and whisper from behind electrical outlets.

Once again, let us define our terms.

THE (RE)DEFINITION OF THEME

Every story is an argument.

A story has a point of view. It has something to say. What it says may be deep, or it may be shallow—and it may be deep to me, but shallow to you, or vice versa. The argument may be intentional on the part of the storyteller, or it may be unrealized. It may even be some mix of the two, as with Shirley Jackson's "The Lottery."

This argument might be simple or it might be complex, though it can often be stated best as a single short sentence. The longer the sentence, the more complex the argument ... and the more complex the argument, the more the story has to do to prove it, and the harder it will be for the audience to connect to it. But if it's too simple, the story might appear simpleminded. Some balance should be sought.

It's not enough to just say a topic and claim that it's the theme. I read once that the theme of *The Hunger Games* is "inequality," but that's not a theme. That's a half-formed idea, an incomplete argument. What is *The Hunger Games* saying about inequality? What is its assertion? What is its point of view on that matter? (More on this in a second.)

Note, too, that the story really *does* have to prove its own argument. In a very real sense, the story's theme works just like the thesis of an academic paper. Even if the theme begins its life in your mind as a question (which is totally fine), by the end of the tale, that question should be answered and the argument made, the narrative having proven the thematic assertion.

And, yes, the proof is made up. The argument is made up. The entire *narrative* is made up, because that's often how stories go. (Stories of a nonfiction nature aren't made up, not really, though in the field of "creative nonfiction" you will find a great many inventive liberties. And nonfiction in any shape can still present facts in a way that draws from a manufactured theme, because (again), this shit ain't math.)

The truth of the theme is somewhere between the author's intent and the audience's reception—you may very well intend one thing, and the audience may very well intuit an entirely different meaning. And that's okay. That's life in the big city. You cannot control what the audience will do with the story once it has been told to them. That's on them.

What's on *you* is controlling the story.

And that means controlling—or at least considering!—the theme.

THEMATIC EXAMPLES AND THREE EXERCISES

Right now, I want you to perform three creative exercises for me. No, no, no, take off the yoga pants and put the sex chair back under the tarp. That's not what I mean. These are purely intellectual exercises for you, the storyteller, to help you frame the power of a fully armed and operational narrative theme.

Exercise 1: Find the Theme in a Story

Pick a movie, a book, a comic, whatever. Any story that you find interesting or intriguing. I want you to take this story, hold it up, shake it around, and see what ideas fall out. What is the story saying? I don't just mean in terms of plot. Can you discern a message? And is there evidence to support the message?

Above, I mentioned The Hunger Games trilogy and how "inequality" is not a complete thematic statement. So, what is? Let's try a few:

"Inequality can only be made right through revolution."

Or: "Rampant inequality turns a world into a dystopia."

Or: "The wealthy use inequality as a tool to keep the poor down."

Those are three themes right there, based on the notion of inequality alone. None of those are *right* or *wrong*—all that matters is that I could reasonably try to prove them with some evidence inside the story. Again: This ain't math. We don't need definite answers; we just need supportable ideas. These three themes are the tip of the iceberg, too. We could conjure themes about power, about voyeurism and reality TV, about love, and on and on. (We'll talk a bit more soon about whether or not a story can support multiple themes, and how it can do that.)

The point is that *The Hunger Games* is saying something. It has a message. It has a distinct point of view, and you can, with some effort on the part of your squishy brain bits, envision that point of view.

So that's the first exercise. Now I want you to reverse it.

Exercise 2: Invent a Brand-Spanking New Theme

Think up an independent theme, unmoored to any story. Imagine any argument you care to make. One sentence, the shorter the better. It could be framed as a question, though it's better positioned as a statement. Here are a few I came up with:

"To defeat evil requires sacrifice."

"Family will always be there for you."

"You really should try to pee before any long car trip."

(That last one is both a theme *and* really good advice.)

You could even take clichés or other sayings and turn them into themes: "Home is where the heart is," or "The way to a man's heart is through his stomach," or "Actually, the best way to a man's heart is with a posthole digger through the breastbone, but if that should fail, consider the romantic power of a reciprocating saw." Pretty sure that last one is from a Hallmark greeting card. Really, any overarching argument or idea—no matter how deep or how twee you want it to be—can work as a theme.

It can be as simple as "True love defeats all," or as complex as "A society cannot truly succeed until it demands equality for all of its citizens, especially those who are most marginalized." A theme can tackle questions about war, heroism, love, hate, sex, revenge, equality, gender, power, travel, identity, bees, spiders, coffee, why that jerk just cut me off in traffic, naps, Lando Calrissian, and—you know what, I'm going to stop now because I think this has really gone off the rails. Point being, when coming up with a theme, it's good to aim for a way to wrestle big topics into alignment with your argument. You're trying to talk about Big Stuff using a Small Story.

And that leads us to …

Exercise 3: Build a Story from Theme

I want you to take *one* of the themes you identified in the prior two exercises. It can be a theme you found in a preexisting story, or it can be a theme you just made up out of thin air.

Now, take that hand-selected, small-batch, locally sourced artisanal theme and use it to come up with a story—a story that highlights the theme and roughly attempts to prove it. When I say, "come up with a story," I don't necessarily mean sitting down and writing an entire novel or film script based on it—obviously, if you want to do that, hey, rock out with your Spock out, you crazy diamond. We'll be here when you're finished. But if you don't want to roll quite that hard, just come up with a short logline (i.e., a single sentence) or short synopsis (one to three paragraphs) that gives the overall cut of the story's jib. We just want a sense of what the story would be, what it would look like, maybe who the protagonist is. Quick cuts.

If you want to get *really* sassy,[3] do this two more times. Come up with two more entirely different stories built around that central theme.

I do this exercise in a lot of my writing classes and talks, in part because I am a fundamentally lazy human being and the more work *you* do is the less work *I* do, and that is a win-win for me. While you're off noodling about themes and story, I'm dicking around on Twitter.[4]

In a seminar, the class lists a bunch of made-up themes, as you have done here. Then, collectively, we choose one to work on. Everyone sits down and comes up with a story around that chosen theme.

My favorite part of this exercise in a classroom environment— and it is a consequence you can imagine right now, using the magical movie theater that is your mind—occurs when writers around the room give the thrust of the stories they come up with. Because

---

[3] Like my buttocks, described on page 100.

[4] Or whatever social media platform is ascendant when you read this: Circleface, Friendzone, Ticklr, etc.

no one story is the same. The *theme* is the same—as in, everyone is working from the common platform of a single theme and singular argument. But the stories that result vary *wildly*. Science fiction here, romance over there, one is a tragedy, another a comedy. Different characters, different situations and problems, different stories.

And that's a beautiful thing. It suggests that theme is like a prism—it breaks a single beam of light into several more colorful ones.

THEME PARK: THE INTERPLAY BE-TWEEN THEME AND CHARACTER

Let's just get this out of the way right now:

No, you don't need to worry about the theme of your book.

It can be a thing you grant literally no thought to, and your book or movie or interactive diner menu can still be good, great, even amazing. All of this theme stuff can hit your brain, and your brain is free to recoil as if it has just licked the back end of a feral cat.

It is, strictly speaking, unnecessary.

Theme is just another tool in your toolbox. Some jobs require certain tools, and other jobs will be complicated by using the wrong ones. Every aspect of writing and storytelling is a thing you must test in your hand—you feel its heft, you test its grip, you look to see what it can accomplish for you—and then you either put it to good use or you throw it over your shoulder and hope you don't accidentally hurt somebody.

Here you ask, though, *Why* would you use theme? Why care?

(And why the hell did I just provide three exercises on theme for you to complete, if it's so unnecessary?)

Well, the reasons pile up if you care to stack them: Theme helps you form a deeper connection to the story, it helps you with a through-line that you can grab hold of to pull you (and the audience) through the tale, it can give the story more meaning, it can be a useful distraction that aids in that most fundamental authorial task (aka procrastination).

But the greatest reason is this:

It grants you additional context for the characters in your story.

Just as the characters are the drivers of plot, so too are they the drivers of theme. *They're* the ones on the page proving or disproving the theme. (Or, less charitably, they are the rats in the emotional and intellectual maze you have created for them, ha ha ha, poor suckers!)

If we pick a theme I made up above—let's say, "To defeat evil requires sacrifice."—then it's easy enough to see who exactly is going to be demonstrating and/or challenging that theme on every page. Spoiler warning: The theme will not be performed and proven by a lamp, or a swatch of wallpaper, or the color blue. *Characters* will be the ones sacrificing. They'll be the ones *affected* by the sacrifices of other characters. Characters will embody the lesson. They will fight *against* the lesson. They will learn the lesson and suffer from it. In The Hunger Games trilogy, the themes—whatever you believe them to be—are forever contextualized by Katniss and, to a lesser degree, by the other tributes, by Snow, by all the citizens of Panem. Different characters may show different facets of a given theme. (In fact, if you try to prove a theme and your proof does not include the character's actions and words, you will have failed to provide that proof.)

The value of theme for you as the storyteller is that it gives you a constant touchstone as you tell the tale. When you're writing a scene, it affords you the chance to ask, *Are these characters acting in a way that reflects the theme?* Keep in mind, the characters are not mouthpieces for theme, but they may be working through the practical realities of it. If the theme is about the costs of heroism, then it's good to write the characters wrestling with that in terms of thought, dialogue, and especially action. Characters should struggle with the ramifications of the theme, even if they don't give voice to it. Just as we don't need to describe the emotion—we can show it, instead—we can show them grappling with thematic implications rather than explaining them. (Or worse, preaching about it. Storytellers sometimes fall into the trap of overindulging theme and making the book into a lecture. Your book is not a soapbox.)

That's also not to say that characters must constantly be wrestling with theme, either. Characters are not slaves to it. They have their own lives, and they do their own thing. But theme provides handholds for you to use as you write the story—and those handholds are for readers, too, as they climb through the narrative.

Look at it this way: We give each character a problem, right? That problem could be anything from the kidnapping of a loved one to, I dunno, *being besieged by bears*. Or, hell, maybe the loved one was kidnapped by bears. I'm not writing your story, so I don't know.

This problem is a more literal, physical problem. It's not figurative. It's not metaphorical. It is an actual problem that the character possesses and must deal with.

The *theme*, however, is like a hidden problem. It's not metaphorical, not exactly, but it *is* more abstract. So, they have the real problem, the one they know about and are in pursuit of … and then they have the hidden, thematic problem, too. It's a problem they may not even be aware of, but just the same, it's one they must pursue. (Or one that will pursue them.) Scene after scene, the theme can rear its head as a problem the character struggles with. And at some point in the story, the character will not only face it—she will face it down for the last time, either confirming the theme or denying it. (And that denial generally means that the theme you thought you had wasn't actually the theme, and that the actual theme was the opposite all along. Which, by the way, is totally fine. Storytelling isn't an act of carving messages in stone. It's writing truth in wet sand, and sometimes, well, sometimes the water comes and washes your truth away in a tide of its own.) Theme provides us with a Grand

Unified Theory.[5] It's like duct tape at a bondage orgy—it binds the whole thing together.

Here's an example: Let's say that the theme of The Hunger Games series is that "war demands a greater sacrifice from those with little power." It teases out a bit of the inequality vibe we were talking about earlier, but also factors in *war*. Now, on the surface, the theme is obvious and it works: Clearly those in power are not the ones committing the greatest sacrifices in the games, in the revolution, or in the war that follows. Not Snow, not Coin. The sacrifices are made by the abused and enslaved. Thing is, that's not Katniss's personal problem, nor is it one she constantly opines about in a theatrical, dramatic way. But it *is* a problem she wrestles with internally. Her initial (personal) problem is that she wants to save her sister's life, and so she steps in and replaces her little sister in the game—but even there, she's setting foot on a path that eventually leads her to war. And the result of that war is one where her sister's life is sacrificed as a result—so, the cost of war is paid, and by someone who had very little power throughout the story.

That's something that doesn't really drive home for Katniss until the end. The theme remains hidden—

Until it's not. And then it's nearly impossible to ignore.

And now, the FAQ.

FREQUENTLY ASKED QUESTIONS ABOUT THEME

I'm framing this as an FAQ because whenever I do a talk on theme, I get, well, questions. And a lot of the questions tend to be the same. Yes, I do groom my beard. Yes, my beard is made of sentient cilia and/or bees. Yes, I would like to eat a taco right now, thank you. And

[5] In simple, dumb monkey terms, The Grand Unified Theory (GUT) suggests that all the physical forces (gravity, electromagnetism, etc.) are all part of one unified force. In this context, I'm saying that the story as a whole is not separate from theme, but rather, unified with it.

those aren't even the questions about theme. I felt that the theme-related questions deserved their own section of this book because this is a sticky subject, one that requires some back-and-forth. It often earns me a lot of questions, so this is ideally a good way to explore the topic.

So buckle in, and let's A some Qs.[6]

Do I need to decide on the theme of my story before I begin writing it?

Nope, not at all. A theme can be *engineered*, or it can be *unearthed*—and that's true of most aspects of storytelling. Sometimes the story is just the thing you tell, and it's only after you finish it that you see all these glittery bits and bobs right there in the dirt. Alternatively, you can enter the story right at the fore with an idea of a theme in mind, and that theme can give your story and its characters focus as the tale unfolds.

I wrote a book called *Blackbirds* about a character, Miriam Black, who can see how you're going to die just by touching you, and—though I don't care to spoil the book—I'll say this: I went and spoke to a very gracious class at Penn State University Erie about the book. It was a Women in Superhero Fiction class, so the students had read the book, and one student in particular brought insight to the book that I had never considered. And it wasn't just that she was bringing up aspects of the book and I was like, "Yes, that's very nice, very insightful, but incorrect." It was a case of her being *spot-on* about certain aspects, and I just never had it crystallized like that for me before. It was as if I'd been wandering around with my eyeglasses on the top of my head for a long time until someone pointed out, "Those should go on your face, preferably over your eyeballs." It was a moment of clarity where I wasn't even the one unearthing something interesting about my book. It had been left to the

---

[6] That sounds dirty, and I apologize.

audience to surmise, and in this case they did an even better job than anticipated.

So that's okay, too.

It's all okay, and that's what makes it all so much damn fun.

Do I need to have a theme at all?

Nope.

I mean, you probably do have one in there. But you never need to name it or even think much about it.

Do what's best for you and your story.

Can I have multiple themes?

Sure can.

Here are a few ways:

1. **HAVE MULTIPLE THEMES.** There. Wasn't that easy?

   Okay, *fine*, I'll give you more. The goal here is to have multiple ideas providing fuel for the characters and the plot they create. It's vital that these themes do not *clash*. In recycling some of our earlier terms, it is far better that the themes run parallel to each other rather than intercut at perpendicular angles—if themes intersect and counteract each other, the story runs the risk of not even having *one* cohesive theme and of feeling at odds with itself. Because it *is* at odds with itself. It'd be like writing a term paper where you're simultaneously trying to prove that vampires exist and that vampires also *don't* exist. You'd have to be pretty savvy to find a convincing middle ground there.

2. **HAVE ONE *GOVERNING* THEME, AND THEN SEVERAL SMALLER, SUBORDINATE THEMES.** Just as you might have a single plot and several subplots—or a single character problem that drives other smaller problems—you can have a larger theme that creates thematic offshoots of itself. So, if you were to say, "To defeat evil requires sacrifice," then a subordinate theme might be "Evil is

championed by the selfish," or "Selfishness is the root of true evil," or perhaps "Evil arises during times of comfort."

3. **ASSIGN THEMES TO INDIVIDUAL CHARACTERS.** I mean, you probably don't need to assign any to the most meager of your characters—that taxi driver who gets a single line of dialogue needn't be a mouthpiece for some big idea. (Though he also *can* be, as a sneaky aside.) Let characters support different ideas and arguments. And here, contrary to the above, it's *okay* for your themes to run counter to each other because often *characters* run counter to each other, too. And which characters triumph and which characters fail will then say a lot about where you and the story fall in terms of which themes are true and which themes fall to the dirt in Thematic Thunderdome.

How hard do I need to hammer home the theme?

Not at all! Don't hammer it home! Remember: This stuff is supposed to be *hidden behind the walls*. Theme is not a giant banner slung above the door—it's a gentle tapping against the pipes, it's a faintly buzzing conduit, it's the skitter-scurry of mice through the ducts. A story ceases to be just a story when it preaches. The audience recoils when they feel like they're sitting down for a lecture. Your goal is not to force them to think, but to gently urge them into thought—not to bludgeon them about the head and neck with A BIG MESSAGE, but rather to whisper it in their ear while dreaming. You're not writing a gospel. You shouldn't be writing an allegory. It's just a story, where characters do things and say things and maybe, *just maybe*, hidden between the lines and buried beneath the text is an idea, an argument, a message.

That said, here's a trick.

It's a little magic trick that sometimes screenwriters use, and that you can use in your story no matter its format.

Once, *just once*, a character in the story can utter the theme out loud. This shouldn't be done in a heavy-handed way—it's not them stepping up to a podium and staring at the audience and saying it in a big booming voice. It happens subtly, in a conversation or as a part of a larger talk. And it happens not in your voice, but in the voice of the character, so it sounds like it's *their* idea and not yours.

Consider: Ian Malcolm in *Jurassic Park* when he says, "Life finds a way." It's an idea persistent throughout the work, even to the point where two "female" ended seatbelts don't fit together, so Alan Grant ties them together anyway.

Or, in *Seven* (sorry, *Se7en*), when Somerset speaks this last line of the film in a voice-over:

> Ernest Hemingway once wrote, "The world is a fine place and worth fighting for." I agree with the second part.

What's interesting about that one is that it takes a literal Hemingway theme and adds its own spin on it.

I'm having trouble figuring out my theme.

That's not a question, imaginary reader, but *fine*, I'll respond to it anyway, despite your flagrant breaking-of-the-rules.

Let me offer some help triangulating your theme.

Ask yourself three questions.

1. What is this story about?
2. Why do I want to tell it?
3. Why will anybody care?

Answering those three questions will show you the margins to the work—meaning, you will see its shape form, like something emerging from a bank of fog. Maybe it's a moose. Maybe your theme is a moose. Did you ever think of that? I bet you didn't.[7]

---

[7] Okay, just for clarity's sake, your theme *probably* isn't a moose.

More to the point, let's say the answers to those questions are, respectively:

1. man's inhumanity to man
2. because I want to explore the dark side of morality
3. because it's politically relevant to current affairs

Then you're starting to see the shape of things. You can be sure that the theme has something to do with how humans treat other humans, maybe how they cloak their evil actions in righteous doctrine, and how this idea is relevant to something actually going on in the news presently—or timeless because it's something that transcends the *here* and the *now*.

What if I have the wrong theme?

That's okay. Like I said: Theme is not math. You may begin a story thinking that it's making one argument, and then, by its end, you see it's made another. As long as it hangs together, it doesn't matter. When we tell a tale, especially for the first time before we revise and redraft, we're wandering through a dark room with only flashes of lightning through the windows to guide our way. We can *guess* at theme, or plot, or how the story will go. But we can be wrong. Honestly, I'm often wrong—no matter how much I outline, whatever I expect to occur, the story nearly always takes weird side journeys. That's okay. It's like planning a road trip. Sure, you plot your course ahead of time. You say, "I'm going to take this highway to that highway," and you print out your map or you let your GPS do the talking.

But sometimes you hit a traffic jam. Or an accident.

Or you come up on an exit and you think, *It looks pretty in that direction. I want to drive by that barn.* Or you see a sign for THE WORLD'S BIGGEST HAY-BALE DINOSAUR, and you're like, *Hell yeah, I need to see that!* So you turn on your blinker, and you take the exit.

You didn't plan for it.

And that's okay, because you get to see a giant hay-bale dinosaur.

SYMBOL AND MOTIF

Let's talk about the literary symbol and motif.[8]

There exists a fairly strict reading that differentiates symbol from motif in this way:

A *symbol* is an image or other sensory component (like, say, a sound or a phrase) within a story that by proxy represents and reflects some component of that story in a metaphorical way. If you look at the mockingjay inside the world of The Hunger Games, it's essentially a bird that exists by a mistake: The capitol genetically designed a "muttation" bird, the jabberjay, who would eavesdrop for them. But the rebels figured this out and fed the birds false information, so the capitol decided hell with it, and released all the jabberjays into the wild—and there they bred with mockingbirds and created the mockingjay, a bird that did not memorize conversations, but *did* memorize sounds and songs. The mockingjay appears consistently in the books and movies, and through the story the bird ends up tied to Katniss, the tribute—the bird is the result of a mistake by the capitol, and so her taking on that symbol both literally and figuratively represents the crimes and errors of the capitol returning to haunt them. (Or, put differently: The chickens have come home to roost.) The mockingjay thus serves as both a literary symbol and a symbol used in the plot of the story: meaning, it's both text and subtext. (Hell, it's the title of the third book. Which one could argue is a little on-the-nose, but that can be okay, especially given that the story is written for young adults, not for a snooty, overly literary audience.)

---

[8] If I were ever to make electronic music, I'd form a DJ duo called SYMBOL & MOTIF, and I would be both the titular Symbol and Motif. One would be the real me, the other would be CGI me, and we'd wear fishbowls and TVs on our heads as we DJ'ed the end of the world. You can buy my album next year.

A *motif* is like a symbol—again, an image or other sensory component—except it doesn't represent just anything; rather, it represents the *theme* of the story in a metaphorical way. It bolsters the theme and delivers on it in an oblique way. Again, in The Hunger Games series, you might argue that the image of fire serves the story as a motif. If we suggest that one of the themes of The Hunger Games is that "Violence can only be ended by violence"—or, to put a different spin on that, "Violence begets violence"—then we are suggesting that violence spreads. It creates itself and feeds upon itself. Just like—hmm, oh, I dunno—*fire*. Fire—which, like the mockingjay, shows up in one of the titles of the books/films—therefore serves as a consistent metaphor leaning into one of the themes of the story. Katniss even manifests this symbol literally, just as she does the mockingjay. And you could argue that the evolution of that motif is one where she thinks she controls it and herself, but in the end she really *doesn't* control it—the violence she looses upon Panem may be essential, but it is not controllable, and it costs her and her family dearly.

(As a fun side note, if you want a mirror of the "fiery mockingjay," look no further than the "firebird" symbol touted by the Rebel Alliance and, later, the Resistance that fights the depredations of the First Order in Star Wars. Then look to the group founded by Albus Dumbledore inside Harry Potter to fight Voldemort, the Order of the Phoenix: Again, you find a bird that, you may note, is very much on fire. Suddenly, we realize that we're talking about the mythological phoenix: a bird that burns up but can revive itself from a pile of ash, used in these stories as a symbol for rebellion and resistance. Which only serves to prove that symbols and motifs give us a very deep, and very interesting, rabbit hole to fall into. Each usage across pop culture is different from the last, while still borrowing from the original mythic source. And this, by the way, is again why originality is overrated in storytelling. No one element needs to be original. *You*, the storyteller, are the singular element brought to the narrative, particularly in the arrangement you choose for the elements at hand.)

The difference between motifs and symbols is important if you're trying to pass a test, but for our purposes the hard separation of the two terms isn't precisely necessary if you understand the two ideas. Instead, simply consider the opportunity to find ways to invoke the themes in your book in metaphorical ways.

Which means it's time we take a little side trip to talk about—

Yep, you guessed it.

Profanity.

Wait, what?

BAD WORDS, GOOD METAPHORS

Okay, we're not *really* talking about profanity—but we are going to use profanity as a gateway to talk about a larger, squirmier part of your story, which is to say, we're going to use it to bootstrap a conversation about *metaphor*.

Profanity, at its core, is often metaphorical in its nature.

When I say, "Dave is a shithead," I do not mean that Dave literally has a quivering pile of feces mounding upon his shoulders. His skull is not poop, nor is it filled with or even covered in poop. I just mean that, *metaphorically*, the guy's got turds for brains.[9]

Words work for us in this way all the time. We let one word or phrase act as a proxy for an idea. That's the awesome part about the human brain—we are smart enough to speak in abstractions. Metaphor is a kind of shared, comfortable lie, right? When I say, "This sucks," I don't mean it is literally vacuuming or slurping something. If I say that, I mean that I don't like it, it's bad, or whatever. It has a distinct negative connotation and doesn't need to be examined any further because we collectively grok the abstraction.

In a literary sense, a metaphor works to compare two unlike things. If I were to say, "His body is soft, like a slice of wet white bread," you would roughly understand what I was getting at. You

---

[9] Fucking Dave.

could probably even remove the lead-in adjective, *soft*, and most readers of that sentence would arrive at a loose consensus of what that means, even if the particulars cannot be agreed upon. (Is he actually wet? Does it mean flabby?) Just the same, the human body and a slice of bread would never actually be confused by anyone who had not first been kicked by a mule. And yet, despite that disparity, the metaphor works, I'd argue, because it finds common ground in abstraction. The metaphor would fail if a) it tried to compare two like things ("that zucchini is like a cucumber"), or b) it tried to compare two unlike things that had no such common ground ("my day was so bad it was like an oak tree"). Too similar or too disparate, and the metaphor will fail.

In other words, metaphors work because we can draw the line between the two unlike things. If that line is too short, it's obvious and underwhelming. Too long, and the line breaks—which means we, the audience, cannot follow it.

Thing is, metaphor doesn't just work at the sentence level; it works as a larger abstraction, too. *Theme* and *story* share a relationship based on the conventions born of larger metaphorical abstraction. When every element of a story lines up to prove and represent a larger idea, we call that an *allegory*. Allegories tend to be religious or moral in nature because a religious text might use storytelling to convey not merely an idea but a hard-coded moral lesson. (Meaning, essentially, an allegory is a fancy lecture. I don't think lectures make for very good storytelling, but your mileage may vary.)

But to a lesser degree, assuming we don't want our stories to become belligerent soapbox preach sessions, we can lightly and loosely invoke theme through symbols and motifs. We show the audience signposts: an image, a sound, a phrase, an action. These are whispers through the cracks—this is us giving hints of what hides behind the walls of the narrative architecture. These abstractions work at a subliminal level because stories are part of a larger artistic frequency: There's the song you hear, and then there's the subversive, subliminal harmony buried underneath. You can't hear it outright. You can't properly identify it. And that is exactly as it should be.

Metaphor is a powerful communicator of both small comparisons *and* big ideas. We can use motif and symbol to bridge the words and actions happening on the page (which take the form of characters building the plot) to our ideas and arguments and identities. And, in that way, they don't just bridge elements of the story to the ideas behind the story—

They bridge the audience to the storyteller.

They connect my story with your story.

That's why theme and metaphor are such powerful abstractions. And why this goes back to what I talked about in the interlude on page 154: A story doesn't merely entertain. A great story informs and challenges. It makes us think, and it makes us feel.

And part of how it does that is by connecting the *teller* to the *told* through the magical wonderful weirdness of theme. It cracks open my chest and shows you my heart. Maybe only for a moment. Maybe only through the smeared lens of metaphor and motif. But it's there.

THE INTERPLAY BETWEEN THEME AND MOOD

Mood is not theme. Theme is not mood.

Theme is that message whispered through the heating vents. It's the seed of the idea that grew into the tree that became the story.

Mood is how the story feels—or, rather, how it makes the audience feel. Mood can shift scene by scene, and, in fact, it *should*: We want to establish a rhythm with mood just as we do in the rest of the narrative. A single gray, grief-stricken expanse of narrative is dull and listless. It's like a song without chord changes. At the same time, neither can mood whip wildly about: We can't go from BLEAK DESPAIR to GIDDY BLISS to GROTESQUE

OPPRESSION to CARELESS LUST from scene to scene, or we'll experience a kind of narrative whiplash.

And here is where mood and theme *can* interplay, should you choose to let them: Theme can be a guide for mood. What I mean is that if you identify a potential theme, that theme can come baked in with moods that are appropriate to it. A theme about inequality should likely at least *ping* an oppressive or bleak mood from time to time, because inequality is rarely going to be a happy topic. A theme about the unconquerable nature of love—well, it would be strange if that theme did not include some positive and romantic expressions of mood, right? Theme can provide a through-line for how you invoke mood and gently shift the tone from one scene to another.

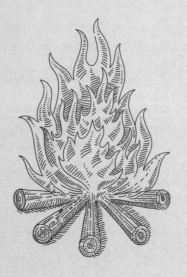

Interlude

THE LAST RULE

Here it is, the corker, the game ball, the season ender. It's the last rule of the book, and it's a rule that's less about how to construct stories and more about *why* we tell stories in the first damn place.

Stories matter.

That's it. That's the rule. It's law, it's holy writ. It's *undeniable*. Stories make the world go around.

Stories can get a politician elected—or bury him after he's in office. Stories sell us products, they convince us of lies or share with us vital truths. *Narrative* is all around us. The entire Internet is made up of narrative after narrative—some of it nonfiction, some of it fiction (and, ahem, some of it is fiction parading around as nonfiction the same way a wolf might shimmy his ass into a set of sheep's clothing).

We tell stories about our families and our loved ones, and we share tales of what happened at work and at school. When we have a bad day, we turn to movies, books, games, plays, and comics. And some of those movies, books, games, plays, and comics will outlive us, and may even outlast our civilization when it's gone and replaced with the next set of people (or sentient cyborg dinosaurs). Some stories come out in their time but speak to us timelessly—*The Handmaid's Tale* or *Casablanca* or the canon of Shakespeare. Some stories are decidedly products of their time, and we use them to understand the period from whence they came.

Stories teach us.

They persuade us.

They *dissuade* us.

Stories are the backbone of mythology, religion, history, sociology, literature. Culture as a whole is composed of countless threads of narrative.

This thing we do, it has meaning. But it doesn't always *feel* that way. When you sit down, and you're about to put a pen to paper to write that next book or short story or script, or whatever it will end up being, you're going to experience that twinge called "impostor syndrome." We all feel it. I get it even still, even after writing over a dozen books and some comics and some film and TV scripts. I get that feeling of being an impostor. I feel like I don't belong, as if I'm secretly a stowaway on a boat that belongs to other, greater people.

And that feeling and fear of being an impostor is just the gateway: I start to worry, what's the point? Who's reading? Who's listening? And somewhere in the back of my brain, I'll hear the echo of that oft-repeated nonsense phrase—"There are no original stories, stories, stories"—and I'll clench up even further. My fingers will pause. My mouth goes dry. I'll feel nervous and anxious and woefully unsure of myself and the mission I've given myself. It happens *every damn time*.

And every damn time, it's bullshit.

Storytelling is not special. I don't mean that as an insult. I mean that storytelling is not some precious, unique thing. The role of storyteller is not a guarded, privileged soapbox. You don't get an official podium with a sanctioned seal of approval. It's not just for *them*. It's for all of us.

Storytelling is a shared tradition. We all get to pass around the talking stick and the magic witch's eye. It's not just for the priests or the chosen few. Telling stories is a powerful common denominator. And listening to stories is as vital and as common as breathing. We are bound together by our stories. We share traits and tales through those narratives—and we also help to spread empathy and compassion and critical thinking through them. Stories are the ripples that carry water from my shore to yours, and yours back to mine. They are a form of echolocation, cultural and emotional and sociological. *Narrative* forms our shared tapestry. You at one end, me at another, and all the threads in between connecting us.

Don't be afraid. You can't be an imposter because storytelling isn't for the few. It's for the many. Stories are for everyone.

Now, here's the last bit of note.

I say that every time I go to sit down and write a story, I feel that fear. I feel blocked, hesitant, *guarded*. That's true now, and I figure it'll be true every day after today until I am kicking up daisies.

But here's what's also true—

The moment I begin to tell the story, that all goes away.

It just *melts*. That's not to say the story I'm telling always comes easy—the first draft can sometimes feel like I'm punching my way through a wall of mud—but the fear? The fear goes. And I start to feel it. I start to *get* it. I connect with something larger than myself, as if there's an unseen river beneath us, a river of song and story into which I can dip my nasty little toes and wiggle them around. It's like any act of stepping into water. At first you think, *oh shit, it's going to be cold, so cold, I don't want to do this*, but then you ease in, and the shock passes quickly. And the water is warm. And it's welcoming. And now you're a part of it.

Push past the fear, is what I'm saying to you. Recognize that stories matter and it is your right and your common human heritage to take part.

Do the work. Tell the tale. To hell with doubt.

Stories matter. They are ours. They are yours.

Now go tell a damn fine story, willya?

Epilogue

AH, HELL, ONE LAST STORY

Growing up, we had all kinds of animals. When I was a wee tot, we had the standard array: chickens, cattle, pigs, a couple goats. My family was a farming family, and my grandfather—who I never met—owned and operated a huge farm in Bucks County, Pennsylvania, and my father took that farm on when my grandfather passed, but not in a full-time capacity. By the time I was maybe five years old, most of the animals were sold off, and we were left with a rotating carousel of farm dogs and cats.[1]

I guess he got to missing having animals around—whether he missed their innocent animal natures or the persistent need to clean up a variety of droppings amidst the cacophony of their many barn-

---

[1] Not a literal carousel of farm dogs and cats, unfortunately. But now I want that.

yard-like sounds, all that snorting and mooing and cockadoodle-dooing. So one day he came home from work.

And he had four geese with him.

Canadian geese.[2]

Those who know anything about Canadian geese know that they are the King Assholes of the Bird World. Some birds are nice, and other birds are assholes, but Canadian geese take the crown and scepter of the Asshole Kingdom. They are loud. They shit green caterpillar-like turds everywhere. They will chase you.

And it's this last point that proved a problem for us, because one day my mother came home from her job in the early afternoon and was promptly chased from her car to the top of an empty gas tank by a gaggle of surly geese. She didn't even make it inside the house—she ran, they ran after, and she jumped up on that big piece of metal in an effort to stay safe from the honking flock of murder birds.

Now, I don't know where my father procured these geese. I do not know *why* he decided to bring them to haunt and harangue our family. But bring them he did, and on that day, they kept my mother up on that old empty tank for three hours, circling her like a tribe of feathered butchers, ready to use their wings to karate chop her dead. (Fascinating point of fact: A goose can indeed chop with its wing, and the rumor is that they could even break a young child's arm with such an attack.)

I was trapped inside the house with my grandmother, forced to watch this.

It is, quite literally, one of my earliest and most vivid memories.

Eventually, my father came home and chased the geese away.

Later, we had a freezer full of goose meat.[3] Which, by the way, is viciously tough dark meat, more akin to steak than to the wan white meat of a chicken, and it requires judicious marinating in soy sauce

---

[2] Technically, "Canada geese," but we don't call them that around here, and it sounds weird so I won't bow to your taxonomy!

[3] A total coincidence, I'm sure.

(not to mention the occasional gentle bite to make sure you don't chomp down on a shotgun pellet and break a tooth).

The geese were a misstep, but from there, my father brought home a series of strange animals for us to raise:

- Peacocks (one killed by raccoons)
- White pheasants (all killed by a fox)
- Guinea hens, which are pinheaded, derpy-birds who will wander into the road and get hit by cars (which these did, and got dead)
- Rabbits (not sure what happened to them, but we didn't eat them)
- Horses (not strange animals, admittedly, but one was named Gretchen and the other named Gremlin, and eventually we sold them)
- A pond full of sunfish, bass, and catfish, all of which my father could summon to him simply by walking to the shoreline with a handful of bread to throw (to my knowledge, the fish are still in that pond even to this day—*perhaps they are even immortal*[4])
- One more chicken, a paranoid white rooster my father brought home just before he left for vacation—a rooster who scratched up my car and crowed at 3 A.M. every morning and who would follow you at a creepy ten-foot distance, tut-tutting at you like a prudish schoolmarm (I shot that chicken with a .410 shotgun, which turns out was exactly what my father hoped I'd do.)

But the most consistent animals on our property were the white-tailed deer. We bought two as fawns, Rudy and Flower, and we raised them in our house until they were old enough to go out to the pen, which comprised a good portion of our farm property, as well as a stable. Those two were like pets, and even at the age of six or seven I could go in there and run around with the deer like they were dogs. They'd come up and chew on your sleeve or your hat. They were sweet.

---

[4] They're probably not, though.

Rudy, though, had a habit of getting out. He'd take his rack of antlers, lock them into the fence, and then give a good corkscrew twist—

He'd open the portal, then he'd waltz out.

Mostly to eat the clover on the other side.

More times than I could count, I would walk outside and see Rudy just hanging out there. When this happened, Dad would go over, grab his antler, and gently walk him back into the pen, then tie up the hole with heavy rope until there was time to replace that length of the fence. One time he ended up going on walkabout, and my father had to wrestle him into the bed of a truck. That required hogtying the deer. Which left my father with a couple broken ribs for it—not because Rudy was violent, but because you really shouldn't hogtie a live buck whitetail. (But, as you have learned of my father, that's the kind of guy he was. Tranquilize the animal? Nah, just rope him like a cow. Doctor? Nah, just cut off the damn finger your own self.)

We introduced a couple other deer in the interim, and as it turns out, deer make more deer, and after several years, we went from two deer to thirty-six of 'em.

We had a whole herd. A herd, it turns out, without much purpose except to stand there and look pretty and eat corn and grass and poop everywhere. Which is their purview and their right, but given that we weren't opening a zoo and—to my surprise—not selling them for food, we eventually got rid of them.

My father sold them to a game preserve.

But again, that itch to raise animals was in him.

So, two more animals came to live with us:

A pair of elk. One cow, one bull.

The cow elk was named Lady.

The bull elk, well, that one my father called Sir Loin.

Yeah, I know.

Thing is, elk are not like whitetails. Whitetail deer are happy, if occasionally skittish, animals. They jump and run and play. Sure, the bucks can get territorial, but raised in captivity they were all pretty pleasant to be around.

Elk are not like that.

Elk—bull elk in particular—are brutes. Or, at least, Sir Loin was. They're big bastards, too—like a horse, if a horse was bristling with musk and muscles and had a skull topped with *siege weapons*. Walking past the fence was like sitting in a shark cage—*bang*, Sir Loin would hit that fence like a Great White. He'd also stand there, stare at you, and masturbate. And here you might be saying, "Well, Chuck, how do elk masturbate?"[5]

I discovered that the elk was masturbating because my father pointed it out.

"See that?" he said.

"See what?" I asked.

He pointed to the elk's undercarriage. "That."

There, the elk was taking his elk thing, his *wanton beastly manhood*, and was aggressively flexing that *turgid bull wang* in such a way that it was flopping up and down like a fish on a dock. It slapped against his belly again and again, and then would occasionally pause to spray fluid.

It was then I realized what was happening.

"He's jerking it," my father said, explaining too late what I had already figured out. And that was the end of that conversation.[6]

---

[5] That or you're saying, "I did not buy this book expecting to be heralded with tales of masturbating elk, and I am not happy." Which is fair, I think. Either way, you bought the book, and here we are.

[6] It echoes one of the earliest and only sex conversations I ever had with my father. I was out on our front porch and he came out, stood there for a little while, then pointed up into a tree. "See that?" he said. "See what?" I asked. "Those squirrels." Sure enough, there were two squirrels, and they were humping with such vim and vigor you had to believe that *they* believed it was their job to repopulate the entirety of squirreldom. My eyes went wide, and my father said, "Always wear a condom," then walked away. So for me, the-birds-and-the-bees was less about birds and bees and more about elk masturbation and the unsafe sex of squirrels.

The elk was an unhappy fixture. We'd gone full circle, it seemed: The elk, like the geese, was a grumpy, violent animal that my father had hoped to tame.

Then came the day I stepped out of my door and I saw the elk standing there.

Not in the fence.

But rather, outside of it.

He didn't see me, so I quickly ducked back inside the trailer. (I had come back home a few years after graduating college, and until I found my own place was living inside a double-wide trailer at the bottom of our property, just ten feet or so from the shark cage—I mean, elk fence.)

I called my father at work.

He said he'd come right home, but I was to "keep an eye on the elk." Reason being, the farmland we once had to ourselves had become developed all around us. All around were houses. In those houses were families. Hell, the very corner of our property was a communal bus stop for schoolkids. I assumed my father was not particularly excited at the thought of having Sir Loin gore a couple of second graders, so he beseeched me to call out of my day job and stand vigil, on "PLEASE ELK DON'T KILL ANY NEIGHBORHOOD CHILDREN" duty.

So, I went back outside and hid behind my trailer, spying on the elk. Where the elk went, I followed, staying at a minimal distance to make sure the musky masturbating antler beast did not catch wind of me. (Turns out, Sir Loin had not sharpened his instincts in captivity. Not once did he notice me.)

My father finally came home, and by then the elk had wandered out behind the old barn, to the back field, where he was munching on grass.

Behind my father's truck came another pickup: It was my uncle.

My father said, "The three of us are going to get him back in the pen."

I blinked and swallowed hard. "What?" I asked. I said, "That can't be right. We should call somebody." I didn't know *who*, exactly. Are there Elk Police? Do we call in SWAT? A sniper? Are the guys from *Jurassic Park* looking for work?

Dad said, "Nah, we can handle this."

Then I looked at his pinky finger, the one he cut off himself, and I thought, oh. *Oh.*

A hasty, ill-formed plan arose.

My father got out three items:

1. A set of my uncle's ski poles
2. A rope
3. A semiautomatic Remington 1100 12-gauge shotgun

He handed my uncle's ski poles to, well, my uncle. He slung the rope over his own shoulder.

And then Dad handed *me* the gun.

Now, I am not unfamiliar with how to use a firearm. I grew up in a hunting family, and my father in his spare time did gunsmithing and got his FFL (Federal Firearms License) to sell guns to friends (and local police), so I knew the ins and outs of this particular shotgun. Just the same, it had been a *while*. I'd gone off to college where, as it turns out, not *once* did I need to hunt up some dinner. I probably hadn't discharged a firearm in a decade.

"I still think we should call somebody," I protested.

Dad ignored it. "If things go hairy and that elk comes at any of us, you need to shoot it," he said. "And it's big, so you'll need to shoot it a few times. Maybe more." He told me to "just keep shooting it" until, I dunno, it stopped killing my uncle and masturbating violently.

The plan was this:

My father would lasso the elk's antlers.

My uncle would prod it with a ski pole toward the back gate of the pen.

And I would shoot it, if it came to that.

And so we approached the elk. We approached this elk the way the nascent paranormal investigators approach the scary librarian ghost in the original *Ghostbusters* film. My father had already tied the lasso like he was a cowboy (*yippie-ki-yay motherfucker*), and my uncle had one ski pole in each hand.

I stood there with a loaded shotgun, safety off, praying to whatever god would listen that I did not accidentally shoot my Dad or my uncle.

Step by step, we encroached upon the elk.

Sir Loin snorted. He lifted his head in alarm. The smell hit me— the musk that came off him was a heady, bestial stink. Like an old carpet soaked in sweat and left out in the sun on a humid day. His fur bristled and his front legs stiffened—a sign he was about to charge, the way he often charged the fence.

I raised the gun.

My uncle got behind the elk.

My father twirled the lasso like an old cowboy.

Whish—the rope looped around the antlers. My father tugged and tightened. My uncle jabbed with the ski poles.

And I thought, *Here we go. We're all going to die. Or at least, they're all going to die and I'm going to have to explain this story to the police.*

The elk, though, didn't charge. He did not move forward but, rather, backward. He reared his head back, resisting the rope—and then with every ski pole stab to the elk-butt, Sir Loin inched forward. My father pulling. My uncle ushering. And me hoping that it would fast come time to put the gun down.

Foot by miserable foot, we walked the elk to the gate.

It was already open. All we needed was for him to go through it.

And then my father did the unthinkable.

He grabbed the monster *by the nose*. He literally stuck his fingers into Sir Loin's nostril holes like he was dealing with an errant bowling ball rather than a *snarling, masturbating hell beast*.

I tensed up. I got the gun to my shoulder.

The elk, cowed, marched into the gate like a truant child returning to school.

My uncle closed the gate. And that was it.

Later—years later, and not months—we had a freezer full of elk meat.

So, that's the story. The last story of this book.

Now, let's take a look at it.

What did I do? What was the shape of it? Did it have a theme? Was there a protagonist with a problem? Did plot take a backseat to character? Were there motifs? Metaphors? Was there a point to be made?

I have no idea. And that, maybe, is the last and final lesson:

I tell this story just to tell the story. I tell it because it happened and because I like it and people seem to like to hear it. I don't tell it to share any great meaning—though I suppose it has a little shape to it (beginning and ending on a freezer full of meat), and I suppose it reflects somewhat the character that my father was (a real do-it-yourselfer, or "thrifty" if you want to put it mildly). You might even argue that the problem that faces him in both this story and the story of his missing pinky finger is a problem that continued on to the end of his life: My father died from prostate cancer, which might not have killed him if he'd gone to the doctor earlier. But he didn't have insurance—preexisting condition clauses are nasty work—and he didn't want to pay out of pocket, and when he felt a lump, he thought himself good enough to diagnose it as a hernia and not cancer. But it was cancer, and a year later, he passed on. He died in my arms, and I felt his last pulse-beat flutter in his neck before it stopped like a broken clock.

Though the story may have shape, though it may have character and theme, I don't tell it for those reasons. I don't share it for any great meaning or reason.

I just tell it because I *hope* it's a damn fine story.

Sometimes a story is just a story. Sometimes you tell it because it needs to be told. Sometimes you don't care about theme or character; sometimes you don't care about tension or pacing. The story is the story, and you tell it the way you know it. And that's okay, too.

Appendix

50 STORYTELLING TIPS

1. If you're bored, we're bored.
2. Remember ABI: Always Be Interesting.
3. Ask yourself the vital question: *Why now?* Why is this story happening now? Why do we, the audience, need to see the story that's happening now—what is the value of us entering the world *at this point in time?* This will help you figure out the shift in the status quo that lead us here. It's not just about an inciting incident, but about the prominence and urgency of the problem.
4. Characters must earn their victories.
5. Characters also earn their failures and losses.
6. If your characters are getting in the way of your plot, *good*. Let them. They *are* the plot. The camera follows them; they don't

move in front of the camera. Assume it's like a documentary: They are the subject, so let the tale unfold in their wake, not in their absence.

7. We care about characters we understand, so it's your job to make me understand your characters.

8. Be funny sometimes. Even if just a little. Even in the most dire, dour circumstances, a little humor goes a long way. It can lighten our load as the audience, and it can further highlight its opposite: The darkness is given sharper lines with a little contrast. We don't understand grief without happiness. We can't grasp the light without the dark. We don't grok hot dogs without hamburgers. Hot dogs and hamburgers are opposites, right?[1]

9. Humor is one of the hardest things to get right in a story. Here's a tip: Jokes aren't necessarily jokes to the characters. What's funny to you might very well be serious to them. A factor of absurdity and contrast can go a long way to making something funny—a lot of the things John McClane does in *Die Hard* are not meant as jokes. He's relieving his own tension, trying to find some kind of tough-guy normalcy in a shitty scenario. It's absurd that he has these one-liners, or paints *HO HO HO* on a dead guy's sweatshirt, or complains about shoe sizes. But it works. In *Jurassic Park*, a dinosaur blows snot on a little girl. It's not funny to her, but it's funny to us because we're horrible people. Ahem. More to the point, we like the silly framing of it—it's a moment of wonder, where she's reaching out to touch a dinosaur with a hesitant hand and—achoo, fffppppbbrt, dino-snot, ha ha ha, stupid child, covered in saurian mucus. Laugh at the stupid mucus child.

10. A scene is multipurposed: It moves the plot, it tells us more about the characters, it dials up or dials back the tension, it sets the mood, it whispers the theme through a keyhole.

11. Characters are not role models, and stories are not lectures.

---

[1] Pssh, don't bring your food snobbery over here. I'm the boss of this book.

12. *Likability* is less important a factor in your characters than *relatability*. We need to relate to them and grok their problem. It's not about wanting to sit down and have a beer with them; it's about being able to live with them for two hours, or a season of TV, or the breadth of a whole novel. Forget *liking* them, but do remember that we have to live with them. If all else fails: Just make them interesting.

13. Interestingness is not only important, but it covers a great many sins. A book can fall down in a lot of places, but as long as it's *interesting*, we will keep on reading. A book with the most nuanced character arcs and finely tuned plot won't matter one whit if it's dull as a dead hamster.

14. The beginning of a story asks questions and answers none. The middle of a story answers questions in a way that arouses more questions. The end of a story is about answering all the questions except for one or two that will keep the audience thinking.

15. The stakes of a story are what can be gained or lost. We must discover them early and be reminded of them periodically—never let the audience forget what's on the table. Something is on the chopping block, and we need to see whatever it is squirming there under the raised cleaver.

16. End scenes *interestingly*. Which is to say, end on a question or an unresolved conflict. Give the audience a reason to turn the page or get past the commercial break.

17. Always hold something back. Always make them want just a little more. Tease satisfaction, but be hesitant to deliver it. This is true for both the characters and the audience.

18. Stories are a combination of entertainment, enlightenment, and exasperation. You want them to be excited, you want them to feel awakened, and you want them to feel emotional.

19. If you're having trouble finding focus for your story or figuring out where it goes, learn the value of outlining. Outlining can look however you want it to look—a tentpole outline, a detailed "beat

sheet" identifying every beat in the story, an Excel spreadsheet. Even when you're in the middle of the story, you may feel suddenly lost—so outline the road behind and the path ahead. Try it. Just goddamn try it. Don't look at me like that. I know you don't want to do it, but life isn't always about doing the things we want and none of the things we don't. I don't want to have to go to the DMV or the post office, but sometimes we just have to swallow our medicine and quit grousing about it. *flicks you on the nose*

20. Reveal too little and the audience will feel lost. Reveal too much and they will feel safe and bored.

21. Safety is the enemy of good storytelling. It shouldn't last. And I mean that *inside* the story, not outside. Please don't chase your audience around with a Weedwacker. Metaphorically, yes. In reality, no.

22. Read outside your genre. Reading only in your genre is how you get the Human Centipede effect (ew, I know, but shut up) where you digest the material and simply, um, *excrete* it back into the story. Nothing new is added. It's just a reiteration of what came before. So read broadly.

23. Also read outside your medium. Storytelling is different in different places, but there are common bones in these ol' skeletons. Prefer novels? Read comics. Like TV? Read a TV script. Play video games? Try to find transmedia experiences and game narratives outside what you find on your Xbox. Identify that shared anatomy. Learn how the bones work and turn together.

24. Characters must make mistakes. But they cannot *only* make mistakes. They must have triumphs, too. A story isn't an endless array of failure and disaster—we must have some sense of success to understand why success must, above all else (and against all odds), not be lost. Further, characters who only make mistakes become intolerable to us. We start to actively root for their failure if we cannot see in them the potential for success.

25. It's okay if your story is therapy for you. Just don't let it *read* like therapy. It's still gotta read like a story.

26. Write confidently. Confidence is engaging. What I mean by that is this: No waffling. The story is assertive—it moves along, it doesn't dally. Everything feels purposeful and driven. If you're afraid, the audience will know. They can smell fear, just like bees and coyotes can.[2]

27. Two simple words add up to one of the most valuable questions in a storyteller's cabinet of mystery: "What if?" When in doubt, ask those two words. Let them unspool possibility. What if this person perishes? What if the plan goes awry? What if you go right when the audience expects you to go left? Challenge yourself and the choices you have made for the characters and for their plot.

28. Treat the setting as if it is a character. No, it's not sentient—it does not have *wants and needs*, but, to go back to what we established in the second chapter, it *does* have problems like characters do. The setting, the storyworld, should have its own problem, or maybe even several problems. Are those problems in line with those of our characters? (Parallel.) Or do they run counter? (Perpendicular.)

29. The best villains are the ones we adore despite how much we hate and fear them. We should adore them, *and* we should understand them.

30. When in doubt, mess with the sequence of events. Change the narrative order of operations. Nobody said a story had to be told in a straight line from start to finish. Some of the best are not. The pieces are movable. So move 'em.

31. When in doubt, mess with the audience. Make them think a character is dead. Give them a dream sequence. Fool them with red herrings. Dangle untruths and misdirection. Let the narrative ground they walk on while reading the story feel dreadfully unsteady.

---

[2] That's just science.

32. Of course, too much of that tinkering and the audience will rebel. They'll find you and beat you with your own book. You can go too far. You can do it too often. Or you can mess with them using a clumsy hand. Trust me, I've done it well, and I've done it poorly. The times I've done it poorly *still* earn me angry e-mails. I see you, CuckWendickSucks69@aol.com.

33. The story is you, and you are the story, but that can't be obvious. You're a ghost haunting the rooms of this house, not an actual inhabitant. Once the audience perceives your presence, the illusion is ruined, the bubble pops, and they'll walk away, uncomfortable.

34. Point of view is our gateway in—both what the characters see, and what they believe. They are the lens through which we view the story. It is through them that we contextualize mystery, conflict, drama, tension. It limits what can be known and what must be known. POV saturates every level of narrative—particularly in prose writing, where the POV affects the mechanism of language and revelation. It's less distinct across other formats: Games may be first-person or third-person (more in line with prose, curiously), whereas comics and film/TV tend to handle it more obliquely. Either way, always think about who is telling this story, who is seeing it, who is *translating* it for the audience. Who is our proxy? Or are they all proxies?

35. A narrative is like an investment. The more you convince the audience to buy in, the longer they'll stay. The more time they spend in your story, the greater their overall willingness to see where it goes. It's like this: In a book, if they read a page, they'll read to the second page. If they read to page two, they're in till page four. The longer they go, the more their investment in the story multiplies. If they make it halfway ... they'll probably finish the story. That's not to say you shouldn't concentrate on making the whole story as amazing as you can make it—but it *is* important to know that you can't count on them staying with you through

a soft opening in the hopes of it getting great later. Tell a great story right from the beginning.

36. Nothing wrong with breaking your story up into segments. Shatter it into its constituent bits. Parts, books, chapters, sequences, episodes, whatever. Maybe you use these so that the reader can see them (PART THREE: THE REVENGE OF FRONG THE DRAGON-MURDERED). Maybe you spackle over the seams so that the separations remain unseen. But a story is easier to envision when it's less a sprawly, monstrous thing and more a thing you can get your hands around. For strangling.[3]

37. Storytelling is often an exploration of cause and effect. Action and consequence. And this is the blood and bone of storytelling. Character wants shit, does shit, shit happens. Character discovers character is not the only character in the world and is in fact in a universe dominated by many other characters who want shit, too. They clash and interact until climax.

38. The climax is the consequence of all that has come before in the story. Everything crashes together. The chickens all come home to roost, except there isn't enough room for all these chickens. Also, the chickens are bloodthirsty zombie chickens. Because I say so.

39. Characters don't know what the plot is. So don't ever expect them to follow it. We can feel when characters are forced from their own program because authors are overwriting them with the Plot Program. It feels gross. Characters only know what they want and what they're willing to do or lose to get it.

40. The audience knows when you're wasting time. Characters act in the straightest line they can imagine. They have a problem, and they aim to solve it directly. Too many stories have their characters uncharacteristically complicate their own quests. That's not to say characters are perfect. Far from it. Their solutions may

---

[3] What? I didn't say strangling. You said strangling. You monster.

be wrong. Their problems may be overwhelming. They can be fragile and faulty people. But we also know when they're wasting time because the plot needs them to. This is the equivalent of padding the word count on your term paper. Don't do it.

41. More to the point, characters are more interesting when they are smart and capable instead of dumb and pliable.

42. Distrust plot formulas or preconceived story shapes. They're useful when they're useful. They're dull, lifeless prisons when they're not. Note that I didn't say *not* to use them. Simply *distrust*. Better yet: Take the formulas you are given, then smash them with a hammer. Rearrange them to see what that earns you, and play with the parts. Rearranging the puzzle pieces will allow you to see if you can make a new, more compelling shape. Formula is safe. We want to be unsafe. Storytellers take risks.

43. A story must feel urgent and necessary.

44. The audience wants to do work. It's why we don't have to do all the heavy lifting. It's why the storyteller doesn't have to give every detail or answer every question. The audience sees the gaps and wants to fill them in—they want to feel invested, like they are a part of the story. How we let them do that is by giving them room to mentally and emotionally invest. So leave gaps. Show them doors you never walk through. Don't overexplain yourself and what's going on—make them come to you. Make them do the work.

45. Storytelling is a series of promises—some broken, some fulfilled. Know which is which, and know why each must be the way it must be. Fulfill more promises than you break.

46. No story is right the first time, and that's okay. The illusion of a stage magician needs practicing. So does a joke or a comedy routine or a song or any kind of performance. A story is a performance. Practice it. Rewrite it until it's right. Don't worry about obliterating the magic. This doesn't obliterate the magic because stories aren't magic, even if they feel that way.

47. The best stories make us feel giddy and afraid—not only when we read them, but when we're sitting there writing them, as well. If you're not feeling anything while writing it, ask why. Take a step back. What will make you care more? What excites you or thrills you? What feels forbidden about the story, and can you make it happen?

48. When in doubt, blow something up. Boom. Metaphorically or literally. Er, within the story. Please don't go blowing actual stuff up.

49. Don't cheat. We know when you're cheating us. When you break the promises of the narrative, when you give us something too easy, when you shortcut the story or force the characters into decisions we know they wouldn't make all for the convenience of story … that's cheating. We can smell it like we can smell a dead fish in the glove compartment. Don't cheat. Take the time. Do the work. Cross all your narrative t's and dot those storytelling i's, damnit.

50. Finish it. Always finish it. No matter how unsure you are. No matter how unsteady it makes you feel. *The only way out is through.* Finishing the work teaches you *how* to finish the work. An ending is one of the most important parts of a story, and you only learn to write them by writing from the start to the finish. Bonus: Finishing what you begin feels good. It gives you a little dopamine release. It offers a tiny widdle *brain tickle.* If you have problems finishing a big story, first try to finish a smaller story. Learn the pattern. Build a ladder out of what you finish. Don't worry about failing. We all fail. The only way you lose is by quitting.

INDEX

WD WRITER'S DIGEST

WRITER'S DIGEST
ONLINEworkshops
WritersOnlineWorkshops.*com*

Our workshops combine the best of world-class writing instruction with the convenience and immediacy of the web to create a state-of-the-art learning environment. You get all of the benefits of a traditional workshop setting—peer review, instructor feedback, a community of writers, and productive writing practice—without any of the hassle.

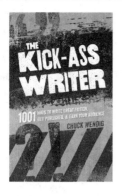

THE DEFINITIVE GUIDE TO CRAFTING A SERIES
The Kick-Ass Writer

BY CHUCK WENDIG

The journey of becoming a successful writer is long, fraught with peril, and filled with difficult questions: How do I get started? How do I write believable dialogue? How do I build suspense? What should I know about query letters? Chuck Wendig will help you ditch your uncertainty, providing gritty advice that will alleviate your fears so that you can find your voice, your story, and your audience—all on the path to publication.

Available from **WritersDigestShop.com** and your favorite book retailers.